"When we Learn from
Someone Ahead of Us,
&
Teach someone behind Us
The road we are on Now
is so much
Better!"
~GB~

Aerial Approach

(Modern and Ancient Pioneers)

Inspiring & CONDENSED

MINI LIFE LEGACY STORIES

Aerial Approach

(Modern and Ancient Pioneers)
Inspiring & CONDENSED
MINI LIFE LEGACY STORIES

Copyright © 2018 G Roai Burnett

Book Design & Technical layout
G Roai Burnett

ISBN-13:
978-0692193686 (GRB GLOBAL CREATIONS)

ISBN-10:
0692193685

DEDICATION

As I read the short mini stories I marvel at the powerful and simply illustrated little snippets that draw me closer to my great ancestors, pioneer family, and friends. Insights and perspectives that would not have been discovered had I not pursued this project. It is said that:

"A STORY NOT WRITTEN IS SOON FORGOTTEN."

I reflect back on a presentation given at a large world family history conference in which the presenter invited his family go back and find a relative that they could relate with and that would have an answer to some of the trials or hurdles they might correlate with our modern day lives.

My heart turns to those pioneers, both modern and ancient, who have blazed the trail before us and paved the way today. Many were found by clicking on their names on the family tree. It was so nice to see that their lives were of great value, even though they might of thought that daily life was very simple, sometimes very difficult, and often times mundane and monotonous. I realized we can learn a lot from each other.. It was fun to share with my family as they were thinking their lives were not all that exciting, but as we hear about it with a little bit of time behind it, we found interesting and fun memories to share with each other. Thank you to all that participated and contributed to this project.

Please forgive me as the book may contain errors hear and their. Hopefully you'll be able to find many hidden treasures a long the way. It's about the stories, so thank you in advance for your patients and forgiveness. "If at first you don't suck seed, (by changing something) you can succeed,"instead of the default of "keep on sucking until you do suck seed" ...Change is Key. ~GB~

FUN
LITTLE
STORIES
OF
(Modern and Ancient Pioneers)

Full of

LOVE
AND
HOPE

~MP~ = MODERN PIONEER
~AP~ = ANCIENT PIONEER
[ ] Very limited Editing to preserve original contribution

ACKNOWLEDGMENT &

CONTRIBUTIONS
(Short stories interspersed throughout the book

After compiling the contributions laughter ensued, then tears came to my eyes as I realized how wonderful and insightful these stories are. I had no idea from the many stories shared, especially some from ancestors that have already passed on that left these little snippets about their lives. This was eye opening. Love was increased for each person as conversations about ancestors, people, places and things that made indelible impressions upon our lives. were shared with love and hope.

I appreciate the support and the spirit by those who have written these contributions. Great thanks go to my dear family for the hours and hours of assistance, even from the badgering, or coaxing, telling me "GOOD LUCK WITH THAT" or. the wonderful strong encouragement too because it was all necessary to keep me moving forward and especially sharing the life lessons along with the fond memories. Thank you all!

It was an honor and a privilege to assemble the contributions into this book and to get it into (digital) print, and especially my older sister for blazing the trail and getting her book completed and allowing me to learn and grow along with her.

~MP~
CHAPTER 1

CPR FOR THE SOUL

--------------------~

Contribution~

Nate Hales Story
(excerpts from his
CPR for the Soul)
I am a 43-year-old agent for an insurance company in
Utah. I became addicted to heroin and other drugs and
began stealing from my father to support this habit. I grew
up in a respected Mormon family, in The Church of Jesus
Christ of Latter-day Saints (LDS), and desperately wanted
to live a cleaner life, but felt powerless over the drugs.
Then one day, I walked up a mountain behind my father's
house and experienced a transcendent, transforming, life-
changing encounter with God that healed my addiction
and helped me gain clarity for the first time in my life.

By the age of 23, I was an addict, such a mess. I was
taking so many pills — "cousins" to heroin...whatever I
could get my hands on. My father is a successful dentist,
and I put myself on his payroll, although he didn't notice. I
was taking checks out of his mail and cashing them. I stole
tens of thousands of dollars from him. His CPA is the one
who realized the money was missing.

There is a beautiful movie called Pleasure Unwoven: An Explanation of the Brain Disease of Addiction. It's a documentary DVD produced in 2010 that explains that addicts just can't stop using, stealing and destroying themselves. I highly recommend it to anyone who has an addiction and anyone who is trying to help an addict. I used to walk to the store and steal things, crying because I couldn't stop myself. That's how bad it was. I lost my car, my job and everything else. I just wanted to die because I couldn't stop this body from walking around to commit crimes just to get high again.

I have an identical twin brother, and we have a younger brother. One day, my younger brother called me on the phone and said, "Dad found out you've been stealing money from him. He's on his way over to your house right now."

I had been in jail a few times, and I said, "I am not going to prison. I'm going to Mexico." So I packed a bag and was getting ready to leave. My dad pulled in the driveway and got out of the car. I began to cry, and I looked at him with dark, sorrowful pity. A horrid emptiness engulfed me. I felt like a damned soul. I didn't even believe in God at that time. My dad was the only latch I had to my old life because my twin brother was using drugs, too. And there he was. I didn't want to get close to him because I didn't know if he was going to try to tackle me or keep me from leaving. I just didn't want to go to prison.

I told my dad, "I cannot tell you how sorry I am. You're looking at somebody who's out of control. I am going to go to Mexico, and I will probably die." In my mind, the only way out was to kill myself. In fact, I had already attempted suicide, but my brother stopped me.

Dad's eyes started to fill with tears, and he told me, "No, no! Just calm down. We'll take care of this. We'll work it out. Don't go anywhere; don't do anything. Just come home. You're going to come home. I'm going to get you out of this deep hell you're in, but you're going to live by my rules. And you're going to go to church with me."

What an amazing human he is. I had already failed at rehab several times and stolen maybe $35,000 from him, yet he took me back in, like the Prodigal Son.

I moved back home, and he wanted me to wake up each morning and read Scriptures with him, go to church with him on Sunday and sit in on the family prayers. I wanted to turn my life around, but I just couldn't stop popping the pills. I started lying to my dad again.

One Tuesday evening, I got back to my dad's house after work, and I wanted to go to a bar or a club. I borrowed his truck and drove to a nearby city to pick up a friend of mine, J.P.. He was a pothead. He loved smoking pot and studying Buddhism. He was into different things every week. J.P. loved going against society and the grain. He told me two missionaries were going to be at his house in a little while to talk to him.

I said, "Let's just go!"

He said, "No, if you want me to go to the club with you, you're going to sit here and wait until these guys are done. I've got an appointment with them."

I protested. "Just leave them. These kids are twenty years old. Why are you going to meet with them? Do you just want to mess with them and tell them Santa Claus isn't real? They're not hurting anybody, and they're not addicted to stuff, so leave them alone. You just want to smoke your pot, trip out on them, Bible-bash them and try to take away their faith."

J.P. said, "No, I don't. Just shut up. Get out of here if you don't want to wait for me."

He was the only person who would hang out with me, so I waited. The two missionaries showed up. This kid from Delaware sat down and started talking to J.P.. Then he turned to me and started lighting up — I can't even explain it. He started telling me about Jesus Christ. I had heard it all before because my dad was religious.

"What Kind of Drug Is This?"
But this was incredible. It was powerful. The Spirit was speaking to me. The young missionary told me, "You are going to change. You're going to influence thousands of people. You're going to do great things — I can see it."

He prophesied my life. The room seemed to glow. I wondered if I was tripping on LSD or something because it was so potent. I wondered, "What kind of drug is this? This light and this hope…" It's like I had been in a dark cave, and somebody ripped the top off the cave, and all this light came pouring down on me. It was a beautiful feeling that went clear through me. I knew what he was saying was true.

The Spirit was burning through the room so strongly. The missionary said, "Can you feel that? That's the Spirit!" Caught up in the overwhelming transformation taking place, he stood up and shouted, "I have never felt it this strong! Wahooooo!"

Something in me changed at that moment. I was still addicted to drugs, but my heart started beating again. The missionary told me, "I want you to go to church, even if you're sedated."

I told him, "I can't do that. It's rude to go to church while I'm high."

He disagreed strongly. So I made a commitment that I would keep going to church with my dad on Sundays. There were times when I'd walk into church, even though I had just popped a bunch of pills. I was like, "I'm here. I'm barely here, but I'm here. I'm sorry I'm wasted. I'm sorry I'm high, but I'm here, and I'm going to continue on this pattern. I am going to turn my life around."

My Mountaintop Salvation Experience:

For the next six months, I tried to quit my addiction and be the man I knew I should be. One day, I got off the bus from work and saw an unfamiliar car in front of my dad's house. I thought it was a parole officer. I wondered if maybe I had forgotten to pay a ticket.

I didn't want to find out. It was 5 o'clock in the afternoon, and I decided to go for a walk, up the mountain behind my dad's house. I saw one of our neighbors, and he asked how I was doing. He said, "I see you at church. Listen, I don't know exactly what you're going through, but all I know is that you've got to give it to the Savior."

I asked, "What do you mean?"

He said, "You've just got to ask Him to take it from you."

We talked for about 15 minutes. Then I walked down the road about a mile. There were no houses out there. My dog, Scruffy, was with me. She saw the whole thing. I looked out across the valley. It was pure daylight, and I got on my knees. I had a conversation with God. I said, "I feel like there's something on the other side. I feel these little pieces of gold that have come into my life over the past six months, like what the missionary said to me. But I can't shake this addiction. I know I'm going to go use pills tonight. I know I'm going to go do whatever I can to just get loaded again. I know You can hear me. I can't do it. You've got to take it from me because I can't do it on my own."

I really didn't want to live anymore. I didn't want to disappoint my dad, who was trying to save my life. I figured I was hooked for life and would die an addict.

At that moment, I felt like someone placed hands on my head. I felt the presence of two people, whom I knew. It felt so familiar. As soon as they touched my head, I knew everything was going to be OK. They felt like brothers. I sensed that they had always been there, had always been in charge and were doing the work of God. Everything was clear. I knew Jesus Christ was the Savior. But the sensation I had wasn't of realizing something; it was a sensation of remembering something, and how could I have forgotten that?

I didn't actually see people standing there with me, but I sensed their overwhelming presence. It was the Spirit testifying. You can't testify about truth and not feel its power. I realized a lot of things that day. When it all peeled back, I remembered that God is so involved in our lives as we're doing our everyday things, and we can't see it. But for a moment, I saw it.

For some reason, I had a pen and paper with me, and I wrote down 20 truths, or lessons, God gave me to strengthen me and overcome my addiction. They were things like, "Don't dwell on anything but the truth of God." The truth of God means that you should work hard to support your family. Another truth is that we should talk good about our neighbors instead of talking bad about them. Just doing good unto others. Everything that's worthwhile, that's where you dwell. That's what you put your mind on.

During this mountaintop experience, I saw my addiction clearly — and it cured me. Addicts know what's going on, but they're so scatterbrained. This experience rebuilt my mind. I stopped taking drugs at that moment, and I never even had withdrawals — no shaking, no nothing. I looked out across the valley, and I saw the intricate involvement of heaven pouring through everything. I felt an inextinguishable love and felt how deeply we are all connected. We are certainly never alone.

A New Beginning
After this phenomenal experience, I walked down the mountain, back into my dad's house. He was there, and I asked him who had visited. He said it was a friend of his. It wasn't a cop, like I had feared. He looked at me. He could tell there was something different about me.

I said, "Dad, I'm going to be honest with you. I have continued to do drugs while I've lived here, but it's gone now. I'm telling you, it's all gone!"

I walked toward him and hugged him. I felt so carefree and happy again, like I did when I was 12 years old. Finally, my brain was in the right place. Everything had hope in it again. Life was beautiful. I went to my room and typed out the 20 truths that God had shared with me on the mountaintop — truths that He had custom-tailored just for me. Twenty years later, I still have that list of the 20 keys to my sobriety.

But even though my brain was fixed, I knew I needed to repay the money I owed my dad and begin serving myself and others as I would serve God Himself. I knew I had to take control of my life, or the devil would do so again.

I decided to go on a two-year mission trip to Atlanta for the Mormon church, the LDS church. I wanted to give back. I wasn't married yet, and I didn't have kids yet. The leaders in the church weren't sure they wanted me to be a missionary. They didn't want me relapsing out there, away from home, and setting a bad example for others.

But then one of the top leaders read my file and told me he wanted me to go. He said, "You've been through a lot."

I said, "Yeah."

And he said, "No, you've really been through a lot!" His eyes seemed to look right to the core of my soul. After only a moment, he proclaimed, "You are going to make a great missionary!" The Lord helped him see, without words, the purification of Christ's atonement.

CPR for the Soul

One day, I was talking to my friend, Greg, a phenomenal guy. I stopped him and said, "Hey, Greg. You have some friends who have gone back to using, but you've always stayed good. Your friends kind of fell back into the pit. They're like the pig that eats its own vomit. How can I avoid doing that?"

Greg told me, "You've got to do three things: you've got to show up once a week and meet with other people, talk about God — you've got to go to church. Second, you've got to pray every day. Show some respect — get down on your knees. You can't be lying in bed. It takes maybe ten seconds or thirty seconds. And third, you've got to read just one verse of Scripture every day. It has to be a meaningful one, and a different one every day. You'll never fall too far if you just do those three things and never miss. The Lord loves consistency!"

Then I realized that those three important activities form the acronym CPR: church (every Sunday), prayer (every day, on your knees) and reading Scriptures (at least one per day). I worked three jobs to go on the mission trip in Atlanta. I went out there and shared with people what I know: CPR for the soul — it's the consistency that counts!
Life Is Grace, and Pain Is a Gift
Life is grace. God has put us on this Earth so we can learn. Every bit of pain we go through helps us understand the object and design of our existence, which is happiness. It is only by His grace that we get to be here.

The pain we feel in our lives is a gift. You cannot comprehend the beauty of daylight and sunshine until you've been in Alaska in the wintertime for three months straight, and you come back down to California and see the green grass and feel the warm sunshine.

To anybody in pain, I want to tell you that we are all in the middle of a process. How do we find truth? It's not that hard, but it is a process. We have to build our spiritual "muscle." If you want to do some pull-ups, you don't just start doing a bunch of them right away if you've never done them before. If you try to skip that growth process and ask God to give you strength without going through the pain, then you have missed the whole point of life. Why would the Lord rob us of the process?
Here are just two of many Bible verses that I turn to when I need to feel God's strength:

"But seek ye first the kingdom of God, and his righteousness; and all these things shall be added unto you."

— MATTHEW 6:33

"For every one that asketh receiveth; and he that seeketh findeth; and to him that knocketh it shall be opened."—

MATTHEW 7:8

~MP~
CHAPTER 2

IT WAS JUST A DRINK
-Shock Waves to Others

~*Contribution*~

Aaron Allen

As I drive this road each morning I contemplate on the marks in the ground which almost became the resting spot of a sidewalk wreath. This morning I had a very poignant thought that became the inspiration for the following message. I wish I could express it as I talked, but my tears would stop me from finishing. Please take a few minutes to read and ponder.

A year ago, I had the privilege of celebrating Easter focused on the spiritual message of Christ and his love for his brothers and sisters as I recovered in a hospital bed. I have learned so many lessons as I have suffered through physical pain and spiritual anguish. I have come to know and believe in Christ at a level that has changed my life and forever shapes me as a man, father, spouse, brother, friend, and example.

"I stand all amazed at the love Jesus offers me. Confused at the grace that so fully he proffers me. I tremble to know that for me he was crucified. That for me, a sinner, he suffered, he bled and died. Oh, it is wonderful that he should care for me
Enough to die for me! Oh, it is wonderful, wonderful to me!" (Lds hymn 193)

The night of my accident exactly a year ago is still a blur; however, I vividly still remember the peace and love of Christ and God that I felt as I awoke and regained consciousness. This feeling was so strong and powerful and encompassed my heart. Oh I wish I could describe how deep, soul freeing, and powerful Gods love for you feels as death door knocks.

I strive each day to stay close to this feeling. It changed me. I plead for all who have witnessed the miracle [of] my life to stay close to God. Believe in him. Believe and live your lives loving and forgiving others. The memories and love you shared with others during this life will fast forward in the present as you stand at the door of death. I am privileged to continue to make memories and be there as a friend for countless others while I fulfill the new mission God has for me.

I am doing very well. My physical infirmities are healing, but more importantly my soul is becoming more Christlike. I have shed tears over the year hoping I can be an example of his love and help you to feel his love. I commit to do my part.

God lives. God loves. Jesus is the Christ and will come again. I can't wait to cry at his feet and say Thank you, Thank you, Thank you!!! I LOVE YOU! I LOVE YOU! I LOVE YOU!

Easter has forever been changed for me. We will all rise again with our Lord, Master, Friend, Redeemer, and Savior. He suffered, died, and was resurrected for YOU!

(The Story Continues)

Sentencing is over and am able to move on to next chapter in life. Here are the remarks I felt Impressed to share at [the court] sentencing.

Six months ago the car wreck I was involved in changed my life dramatically.

The worries and pain of my physical infirmities will be with me and my family for the rest of my mortal life. The financial burden that my family may face due to my early potential death may become a challenge. The stress and impact on my wife, children, and family the past few months are hard to quantify let alone put into words.

With these challenges it would be very easy to be bitter and vindictive against [this impaired man]. However, from the moment I came to full consciousness a few days after the accident I have felt a different spirit. I found a spirit of gratitude to be alive. I found Jesus Christ's spirit of love and look forward to being with family, friends, and a community that loved me for a few more years. But, Most importantly I found the spirit of Christ's atonement and mercy in forgiving me of my sins and my ability to forgive [this man] for causing some setbacks.

I was humbled by the many prayers offered in my and [the impaired driver's] behalf. My children's and wife's prayers for his recovery touched my heart. We continue to pray for his ability to recovery from alcoholism and pray that he will find peace in following the Lord.

My recovery has been a miracle. The events of that night and the participants placed in the experience were not there by coincidence . I stand before the court this day to boldly exclaim that Heavenly Father, Jesus Christ, and the Holy Spirit are real. There is life after death. The peace and love in that location are worth living a good life on the earth. My life's mission is to be an example of Christs love for all others to feel. I will go to my grave helping others know that they are unconditionally loved by the Lord.

[Looking to the drunk driver:] Please take this time of temporary setback and put your life in the ultimate direction you want it to go. Honor the men and women in your life that love you and prove to them that you can live a life full of love and compassion.

Thanks to my family members, doctors, and nurses who spent many nights tending to me and helping me recover from the many injuries. Finally thanks to my dear wife who has been by my side through this entire experience. I will be forever indebted to her and the example she set for our beautiful three children. Her name will be honored and revered for eternity.

~AP~
CHAPTER 3

WASTE BASKET ARTIST
One person's garbage is another person's treasure.
Grandma Margie Boyle

Life history of Margaret May Warner Boyle

Was born on March 16, 1917, in a small single house on 20th St, a block from Washington Boulevard. We lived about a block from town, a short walk to the center of town. The little house is still there, but I was born in. When I was born. The doctor failed to register my birth with the state and legally I was nobody until I had to obtain a passport for travel later on. Then I had to do considerable research in order to obtain a birth certificate.

My dad, James Livet Warner was a dedicated railroad man. He carried a little grip-like suitcase, and we would always run to see what he brought home for a treat. It was usually pack [of gum]. The neighborhood kids always liked him real well because he was generous with his gum.

Dad spent four days on the railroad and two days at home continuously until his retirement, after 51 years of service. He was extremely loyal and faithful employee and would not allow us children to say anything negative about the railroad claiming. "We should not bite the hand that fed us." They gave him a nice TV when he retired. They had his picture in the railroad magazine with a nice write up.

Dad collected , diamonds, but it didn't do him much good because they were all stolen. When they came home in 1939. Someone had ransacked their home and taken all their valuables.

My dad was 30 years old when he married mother, who was 20. My mother, Margaret Elizabeth Harbertson Warner, was a tremendous homemaker. She had a strong testimony of the truthfulness of the gospel. She had a little library church books. She would bring some of them out to renew her memory of the Scriptures.

My mother was an excellent cook and so was my dad. I remember their homemade stew and soup and Chile, and mothers pies and cakes. Mother could make the best layer cakes I ever tasted. It was like velvet. Dad was an expert on stews and soup.

My parents would take me, when I was in the only child, to the vaudeville and show at the old Orpheum theater, and to dinner afterwards.

I had two boy brothers die in infancy. One in 1918, Lester Lamar Warner of the flu, which was a terrible epidemic in the city at that time, and children were dying like flies. My parents, myself and the baby all had this flu, and they said it was a blessing that I ever survived. Two years later, Ray Harbertson Warner arrived. He was a healthy, beautiful baby. At 4 1/2 months. He died after the doctor lanced his ear after he had a sudden earache.

Mother was terribly upset at this, and was too nervous to stay alone, so we moved to grandma Harbertson's home. We stayed a year until she was able to face life again. That year, remains in my memory as a very choice experience, including sleeping on a feather bed and also having my Christmas sock hop on their old-fashioned wall telephone by their big heatrola in their dining room. On the side of the dining room was couch fitted with a feather bed mattress with which I sunk into literally, and greatly enjoyed on the cold winter nights. I had the privilege of becoming very close to my grandparents, whom I consider [to be] the salt of the earth.

My Grandmother, Mary Elizabeth Moffat Harbertson was married to John William Harbertson. Grandma was a [avid] reader, she read all she could get a hold of, and was a refined, sensitive little lady, who was a super cook. She had her own flower garden and presented all of her visitors with a bouquet of her beautiful flowers and [a bowl] of her homemade chili.

Grandpa was a farmer at heart, who [had] choice, vegetables, and [shared this passion] with each of his sons, who built the Harbertson Ford Motor company, located in the northeast corner of Washington Boulevard. On the second floor of that building was a sports arena and a wrestling school. The children included John, James, Brigham, Perl, Mary, Margaret, Edna, and one child that died in birth. Grandpa liked to read and he carried a doctrine and covenants around with him, and he had memorized most of it. He would say, "Margie what chapter would you like me to read." And he would recite it. Uncle Jim invested his money in farmland and he had grandpa Harbertson farm it. He had a farm with cows, horses, and a chicken coop and chickens.

When I was six years old, my sister Lois arrived. She was born in our home at 865 27th St. She was a beautiful, fragile baby who had lots of ear infections. Consequently was a bit spoiled, because mom was a bit cautious because of her previous experience with the baby boys.

At this time in my life. There was a family who moved two doors from us to have three little girls close to my age. Their names, Rosemary, Glenna, and Doris Dee. I was extremely happy with the companionship of these three girls, and brokenhearted when they moved three years later.

I entered the first grade and had a teacher that scared the life out of me the first year. The second year, I had a lot of sickness and was absent from school. The teacher wanted me to repeat the second grade. Mother put her foot down and insisted I would hold my own in the third grade. Evidently I did, as the teacher in the third grade suggested that I skipped the fourth grade, Mother refused. The sixth grade teacher wanted me to skip the seventh grade. She came over to our home and I listened through the crack through the kitchen door. I was very disappointed in this, as I wanted to to be a classmate of my cousin, Jim Lazenby.

Many of my fun experiences as a child, were the picnics that were planned with Aunt Blanche, Aunt Date, and Jim (Aunt Blanches Son). Many enjoyable afternoons were spent at the railroad men's boardinghouse ran by my Aunt Date (my dad's sister, Caroline Warner Lincoln). She was widowed after eight years in Randy's boarding houses for survival. I remember her white linen tablecloths, and her tempting meals served thereon. She was very nice to us when we visited, and always would have us have dinner and send up to the drive-in for a picture of cold root beer to have on her front porch. Once in a while, when I left, she would put a silver dollar in my hand.

When mother had the twins. She was swollen up. After my mother had the babies, that was really shocked when we met him at the door and told him he had twins. He was so thrilled! We had waited until two o'clock in the morning to tell dad when he came home from the railroad.

When I was 12 1/2 years old, we moved to the brand-new home at 2030 Fowler. The homes and in that area. had been purchased by families. One time I counted 90 children on our block, so my life was fun, fun, fun with all the kids, but I don't know about mom and dad's. At this time I made one of my choicest friends, Dorothy Russell. After high school, Dorothy's life was not too happy, and I have completely lost track of her.

In high school art was interesting to me, and I got excellent grades in this subject. [There] was a Christmas lighting contest, and it was [to draw] a large sketch of the first security Bank building, including a Christmas lighting design that I had planned. It really irritated me to draw the sketch. Finally, I just crumpled it up and threw it in the wastebasket. Two weeks later, in the Sunday paper, my dad came into the bedroom and said,
"Look at this!"

I had won first place and a check for $10, included in the letter from the bank. My teacher had retrieved it from the garbage, smoothed it out, and entered it in the contest for me. Boy was I thrilled! I was jumping up and down on the bed!

~AP~
CHAPTER 4

GEORGE WASHINGTON HILL
(5X) Great Grandpa

NEW BEGINNINGS

Moving, Moving, & Sick to Death & MOVING

INCIDENTS IN THE LIFE OF GEORGE WASHINGTON HILL (By himself) (Retyped by Edith L. Baker, 2003 and retold by 5X Great, great great great grandson & indian 4 Corners missionary -G.B. (Family Tree)

Ogden City, January 2, 1878

The writer of this narrative was born on Federal Creek, Ames Township, Athens County, Ohio, March 5, 1822, of poor but honest parents. My father, Richard Hill, being a mechanic and working at his trade of stone and brick mason, caused him to ramble about a good deal.

At the early age of four years, I was sent to school. My first teacher was a woman by the name of Betsy Bebee, to whom I went my first quarter in the town of Athens, Ohio, where I succeeded so well that I went nearly through the old-fashioned Webster spelling book. My parents were Methodists of the strictest order, my father being a class leader in the Methodist Church. The ministers always stopped at our house as they passed around on their circuits, and my being rather forward for a little boy, they made a great deal of me and took a great deal of pains in teaching me the doctrine of the Methodist Church. In this way I was raised strictly a Methodist, although I never joined their church.

At the age of six, my father moved to Sandusky City in hopes of finding steadier employment and better pay. But with better wages came heavier expenses, and having to associate with all kinds of people he became addicted to drinking and spending his means in that way, and seeing no prospect of bettering his condition, we finally moved back to Athens County where I was born. Here he bought a farm and thought to settle down and stop rambling, but he was not really satisfied as this was a very poor country–hilly, rough, broken country–and poor land. Consequently, on the return of my uncle, William Hill, father's brother, from Galena, Illinois, with glorifying accounts of the Illinois country, my father got the Illinois fever and it carried him off to Illinois for a short time. We remained in Paris, Edgar County, but in the fall we moved out into Coles County on the Little Embarros River in as beautiful a country as I ever saw, and bought a farm.

We now imagined ourselves at home. We had as beautiful a place as I ever saw, one-half good timber and the other half as good prairie land as ever laid out of doors. In the spring we set in to making brick with a will, thinking that we had got to the right place at last, but with the commencement of summer came the chills and fever and we were all down with it, insomuch that we were unable to make but two small kilns of brick of fifty thousand each in the whole season. We were in this condition when my Uncle William came along and advised us to get out to Sangamon County, assuring us we would be healthier.

So Father took his advice and broke up again and moved to Sangamon County. Here he bought another farm of one hundred and sixty acres in the timber of Sangamon River, ten miles east of Springfield. Here, as soon as spring opened, we went to work and put in about forty acres of corn and some other crops and then turned our attention to the brickyard. As usual, everything seemed to prosper with us until summer again came, when all hands came down with the fever and ague. As usual Mother came down with it so bad that it seemed as if she would die.

Anyhow, Father now declared he would leave the prairie country for good, so we packed up our traps and started back for the state of Ohio, leaving two kilns of brick of one hundred thousand each standing in the kiln untouched. Some forty acres of corn was left standing in the field uncared for, besides a good deal of other stuff, none of the family being able to drive the team but myself, and I was shaking with the ague every day.

In this way we traveled along until we reached the Wabash country. By this time Mother was so bad that Father thought if he continued traveling, he would lose her, so he concluded to stop for her to recruit, but she continued in her bed until cold weather, when he decided to stay all winter.

During the winter we all got our healths good and Father, thinking it would not be very sickly in the timbered country along the tributaries of the Wabash, he went into Clark County, Illinois, and bought another farm. We stayed in this neighborhood until I was about twenty years of age, but still were not satisfied. My oldest brother had married a young lady by the name of Rhoda Wheeler and had moved in the fall of 1841 to the southwest of Missouri. He continued to write back what a good place it was, when in reality he was only homesick and was not able to get back. Finally, in the spring of 1842, Father took it in his head to move out there, so we sold out for what we could get and in the month of June we started for the new country where it was represented people could not get sick. But of all the moves we ever made, this was the worst move we ever did make, for it was a very poor, barren, rocky, hilly, rough country, and it was certainly the sickliest country I was ever in. We had not been here but a short time until the sickness commenced. People here would take congestive chills; some would die in the first chill; most would die in the second, and I never knew of but one person that lived over the third and that was myself, but I presume I was as near my last end there with that complaint as I ever was in my life. I believe today that the only thing that saved my life was that I had not done the work yet that I had come to do. It was the chills left me in such a fix I was unable to do anything all winter. It seemed that I had split my breast bone in two and it would not unite until the warm weather in the spring. Still, we remained here until the summer when Father took ague. He became so impatient that we broke up at once and started back east, determined to get out of so much sickness, but in this we were foiled as in many other things, for we had only gone about 60 miles until Father got so bad that I refused to go farther until he would get better, for I knew if we continued to travel he would die.

Accordingly, we stopped in Dallas County to wait for his health to get better. Finally we rented a farm and stopped. It seemed that there was something in my destiny or something else that would not permit me to return to the east, for every time we would start and try to go east, sickness or something else would compel us to stop, so that I concluded to give it up and try and become reconciled to the west, let what would transpire.

~AP~
CHAPTER 5

GEORGE WASHINGTON HILL
(5X) Great Grandpa

GORGEOUS GIRL & THE CURIOUS BOOK

What we do for Love

Finally, in the spring of 1845, I bought two small farms on the Little Me Go (Niangua) [River] and thought that I would settle down for a time at least. One of these farms was designed for Father and the other for myself. It was here that I became acquainted with an estimable young lady by the name of Cynthia Stewart, and having bought a farm for myself with a house upon it, I began to cast about me for a partner to put into the house to keep it for me, and thinking that I had found in Miss Stewart my partner for life, I proposed to her. Her answer was that she was a Mormon and that I did not want to marry a Mormon. I told her I thought Mormons were as other people. I believed Joseph Smith to be an imposter, but for all that I thought just as much of Mormons as anybody else. She gave me "The Voice of Warning" by Parley P. Pratt to take home with me to read and then see whether I would think the same.

I took the book to read, not thinking to find in it anything that would be of interest to me. I was always a great hand to read and had always had a practice of reading all kinds of books that I could get a hold of. But what was my astonishment to find that it claimed a perfect organization of the Church of Christ with apostles, prophets and all other appendages that belonged to the church anciently and that I fully believed it would take to constitute the Church of Christ in any time. When I found that they made such bold pretensions and claimed that the church was organized with all the gifts and blessings as was the church anciently, I became so interested in the book that I read it over and over again and wondered if I really was living in a day when the church was again restored to the earth.

I pondered the matter over in my heart, the spirit all the time bearing witness to me that the work was true. I resolved in my mind that I would go and see for myself. I had always, from a child, believed that it had been my lot to live when there were apostles, prophets and teachers upon the earth, when there were men upon the earth that did commune with the heavens, that could obtain the word of the Lord for man, and when I learned that the Mormons claimed to be that people, I determined to investigate it for myself, and if I found on investigation that they really held the priesthood, that the angel had already visited the earth, I determined to cast my lot with them.

But what should I do now? If I told her that I loved her and that I believed in Mormonism, she would say, "You're a deceiver; you profess to believe in Mormonism just to get a Mormon girl for a wife." I concluded that I would tell her that the book was well written and that it contained good doctrine and so on and pass it off in that way, and that I would conceal my feelings from her. But I was not allowed to deceive her for any length of time, for in a short time a circumstance occurred that compelled me to show my true colors.

Sometime before this there had a Campbellite preacher come into the neighborhood and commenced preaching, and we had attended his meetings regularly every Sunday from the fact we had nowhere else to go. The preacher construed our regular attendance into conviction and made his brags that he was going to catch that young Hill. He said that I attended so regularly and paid such good attention that he was sure that I was converted. When I heard of Gordon's bragging, it riled up my feelings a little. If treating him with respect, as I had always been taught to treat all denominations, would be taken for conversion, it rather riled my feelings. Still, I attended his meetings, and on the following Sunday between meetings I was seated at the table looking over the Testament when he came over and took a seat beside me and tapped me on the shoulder. "That's right," he said to me. "Study the scriptures, for in them ye think ye have eternal life, and they are they which testify after me."

He continued in this strain until I became a little vexed with him. Still, I was a little afraid of him, for I thought that a mere boy and unpracticed as I was, I could not think of what I wanted to say and he would have the advantage of me. But his simple, foolish talk finally overcame my fears and I concluded to ask him a question that I knew he dare not answer without equivocation. Says I, "Mister, allow me to ask you one question." Says he, "A thousand, if you wish."

"Says I, "One will do, and that is, when you were preaching today you quoted the Savior's charge to His disciples when He said to them, 'Go ye into all the world and preach the gospel to every creature. He that believeth and is baptized shall be saved, and he that believeth not shall be damned. . .' and there you stopped. Now the question is, why did not you go on, quote the charge in full? '. . . and these signs shall follow them that believe,' and so on, in order that when we found believers, those that had the Gospel of Christ, that we might know, for in these signs there was a test that we might know beyond the possibility of a doubt when we would find true believers, for the Savior declared emphatically that these signs should follow them that believed." This brought on an argument.

He became so excited that he took the floor and walked the floor and talked the whole time insofar that I could not get a word in edgewise. This, I told him was not fair, that if he wanted to argue the case with me, that half of the time belonged to me, and on account of my bashfulness, I suggested that we retire to the mill to ourselves where we would not expose our ignorance. Here I found out he was as afraid of me as I was of him, for he took me up in a moment and we retired at once. Here we had our argument to ourselves as we supposed, and I used him up, insomuch that he acknowledged to me that these blessings were not in the church and that they really were not the Church of Christ, but said that it was the opinion of their head men that they would finally come to the standard and would finally have those gifts and blessings in their church, but said they did not exist on the earth.

On looking at his watch, he found that we had argued so long that it was already twenty minutes late, so we were obliged to stop after his acknowledging me to be in the right. When we opened the door to come out, lo and behold, his whole congregation were there. They had been eavesdropping us and overhearing his acknowledgments, which so disconcerted him that he did not know what to do. They formed a circle around us and marched us to the house in the center. When about halfway to the house, he made one of the most foolish remarks that I had ever heard. Says he, "Mr. Hill, there is one passage in scripture that very few people understand." "Aye," says I. "What is that?"

Says he, "It is the two witnesses spoken of by John." Says I, "What of them?" "Says he, "They are simply the Old and New Testament. The Almighty never did nor ever will give any other witness to man."

Says I, "Mister Gordon, did or ever will the Old and New Testament live and prophesy in the streets of Jerusalem for three years, do many wonderful works, even to call fire down from heaven in the sight of men, visit the earth with plagues as often as they will, and finally their enemies overcome them and kill them and their dead bodies lay in the streets for three days when the spirit of life would return into them and they would stand upon their feet and would ascend up into heaven in the sight of men?"

Says he, "What is that?" I repeated it over to him. Says he, "Mister Hill, I must see you again. Meet me here next Sunday and we will have this matter out in public." Says I, "All right, Mr. Gordon, I will meet you."

Well, he went into the house and called the meeting to order, sung and tried to pray but could not. He got up and undertook to preach but could not think of anything to say, and in a very few minutes he dismissed the meeting.

I now thought I had surely got myself into it, but determined not to back down. I went and prayed in secret to my Father in Heaven for assistance and that He would not desert me in the time of need, and I would defend His cause well. I went to work all the week taking notes and preparing myself for the encounter that I thought was sure to come off on the next Sunday. Having prepared myself as well as I could, I repaired on Sunday to the place where I supposed I was to meet the champion. But lo and behold, he never came, although he had been preaching there every Sunday all summer and had baptized about fifty. He deserted his flock and his cause rather than to meet the truth, although in the hands of a mere boy.

This debate served two purposes: One was, it served to strengthen me in the truth and to strengthen me in my determination to gather with the Saints, for, thought I, if the truth is so potent that in the hands of a mere boy it can subdue their veterans, it is something worth striving for. And the other, it had revealed my true position so that it was no longer worthwhile for me to try to conceal my convictions.

So, I resolved to marry and gather with the Church. Although my father had recommended Miss Stewart very highly to me in the first place, yet when he learned that they were Mormons, he did everything he could to discourage me by telling me all manner of tales that they were accused of as a church, although his prejudice against them was all caused by hearsay and lies from their enemies, as he had no acquaintance with them whatever, knew nothing of their doctrines, but allowed himself to arrive at conclusions from reports from their enemies. But I reasoned with myself that it was me that had to live with my wife and that I had to work out my own salvation, if I had any.

I determined to carry out the resolutions I had formed, and on the eighteenth of September, 1845, I was married to Miss Cynthia Stewart. A Methodist preacher by the name of Yeager performing the ceremony. I had gone some twenty miles to get him to marry me, as I did not want a justice of the peace to marry me.

As Yeager and I were on our way in, there was an incident which occurred that I shall never forget. He asked me where I got the arguments I used against Gordon in our debate at the meeting, as he was there and heard it. I told him from the scriptures. Says he, "Did you never hear the Mormons preach?" I replied, "I did not." Says he, "You advanced true Mormon doctrine."

I asked him if he had been acquainted with the Mormons. He said he had heard Joseph Smith and Sidney Rigdon preach. Says I, "Do they preach a good doctrine?" Says he, "They preach a doctrine that no man can refute." I, thinking to lead him on a little, asked him what he thought of some propositions I had made to Gordon. He said he was very much like the learned Dr. Johnson that he did not know anything about. He never said anything about this; still, it served to strengthen me and show me that Yeager was preaching a doctrine that he did not believe, as well as Gordon.

Well, after all of the prophecies of my people as to what would be the consequence of my marrying a Mormon, the wife of my choice has always under all circumstances proved a good and faithful and true wife to me, and I have never regretted my choice but have always considered that I had one of Heaven's greatest blessings in her.

~AP~
CHAPTER 6

GEORGE WASHINGTON HILL
(5X) Great Grandpa

FORSAKE ALL-

Leave Mom & Dad

Carve a new destiny

At the time I was married, I was more the subject for the doctor than for the bridal chamber. I had had the chills and fever and bilious fever and intermittent fever all summer, and the day I was married I had started from home in the morning without eating anything and had rode on horseback between forty and fifty miles without taking food or drinking anything but water, and sometimes I almost despaired being able to sit on my horse until I should get home. However, I was able to hold out until we arrived at home, but I was as dizzy headed as if I had drunk a half-pint of whiskey, although I had not tasted of liquor for months and I do not know as I had tasted it for years. In fact, I had become so disgusted with seeing men drunk and wallowing in the mud and quarreling and fighting and abusing their families, bringing ruin and disgrace upon themselves and everybody connected with them that I would not taste of the stuff. Although I had made hundreds of barrels of it, I would not taste of it. Still, on this occasion I was really as drunk as if I had been drinking whiskey.

I had now made up my mind to leave father, mother and all my relations and friends according to the flesh and to carve out a new destiny for myself in a strange land and among a strange people, believing firmly that my God would not forsake me and believing the Savior's saying true where He said, "He that will not forsake mother and father, houses and lands for me is not worthy of me."

I determined at once to make the sacrifice. Accordingly, I commenced to lay my plans, and believing it to be the best to go up to Nauvoo for instructions, I made my calculations accordingly and appointed a day to start. But it seemed that was not the thing to do for before the day came I would shake so hard with the ague that I would put off the time to start until another day. This was repeated three times, when I came to the conclusion that it was not for the best for me to go to Nauvoo that fall, and so gave it up until spring. In the meantime I learned of the exodus from Nauvoo into the wilderness somewhere, but where I did not know.

This determined me to sell at any price and accompany the Church at all hazards. My mother-in-law also requested me to take charge of her affairs and dispose of her property as well as my own and bring her and her family of nine children along with me. This was rather more than I had bargained for. I proffered if the boys would come along and take charge of their own affairs I would render them all the assistance in my power, but they refused, saying they would not assume one particle of the responsibility of bringing such a family into the wilderness to starve, but if I would assume the responsibility and take charge of the affairs, they would assist. I finally consented, thinking I would undertake any hardship rather than to leave my mother-in-law behind when she was so anxious to come.

So I went to work and sold out our possessions for what I could get, which was a mere trifle—not one-fourth of what they were worth—settled up all her business as well as my own, and in June, 1846, bade adieu to home and friends by the ties of nature, and launched forth into the wide world with a large family to see to and very little means to see to them with, but placing my trust in God. Like Abraham of old, I started forth to a strange land. I knew not where, but determined to find the Church of Christ and identify myself with it, to cast my lot with theirs, come weal or woe. It did not matter with me if I knew I was right. I did not care what country I got to if I was able to find the Church.

We took our course for Warsaw, thinking that by the time we had crossed the Osage River, we should be able to learn the whereabouts of the Church. In this we were disappointed, for we could not learn anything definite about them, only that they had left Nauvoo for the wilderness. I knew they were north of us somewhere, so I determined to steer north until we would strike their trail, and I knew that once on their trail we could follow them up, so we turned our course for Boonville, crossed the Missouri River at that place, still getting no tidings of the Mormons. We passed on up by the way of Keitsville (Keytesville, Charlton County). Sometimes we would hear they were up in Davies County, sometimes that they were already out on the plains. Getting so many reports, and no two of them alike, we hardly knew what course to pursue.

I was musing on these different reports as we were traveling along in a big plain road when we came to where there was a dim road turned off to the right, like an old wood road that did not look like as though there had been a wagon on it for a year. But I did not want to travel the course we were going, now we had got across the Grand River. I felt all of a sudden as soon as we crossed the river that I wanted to go more to the right, and as soon as my eye caught sight of this road, the spirit seemed to say, "Take that road." I turned my team into it and went right along without asking anybody where it went or how far it was to the end of it. After I had taken this road, I was satisfied again with our course.

The same evening, the little one-horse wagon my mother-in-law rode in broke down, every spoke in one hind wheel breaking. We now seemed to be in a fix. There was no blacksmith nor wagon shop in twenty miles of us, as I knew of, but I thought there had to be a first time to do anything, and although I had never done anything of the kind, I knew we could not stop there to hunt for somebody that knew how to do such work. So away I went to a field that happened to be in about a mile and got a rail out of a fence and went to work with a dull axe, a dull hand saw and a dull drawing knife, which was all the tools we had, filled the wheel, put on the tire and started on in one day, thinking I had done very well in my first attempt at wagon making. Although I had seen nicer jobs done, still it answered our purpose very well. I had this job to do twice that summer, but after I had performed my first feat, I did not mind it, for I thought I was getting to be quite a wagon maker.

After following this old road some forty or fifty miles, it brought us to Kelsey's Mills. Here we got the first correct information that we had had at all about the Mormons. We learned that they had established a resting place about eighty miles from here [which] they called Pisgah. We learned also that it was the counsel to exchange our horses for oxen as they would travel better on grass than horses. This suited me and seemed to be good counsel, so we stopped here one week, trading our horses for cattle.

Here were the first Mormon elders that I had ever seen. Their names were Thomas Workman and Samuel Brannon. They went with me all around the country and were of good service to me, assisting me to trade. Resting here for a week was also of great benefit to my wife as her health had been very poor for some time [she was pregnant].

After having finished our trading, resting one week, and obtaining supplies, we resumed our journey. A few days brought us to Pisgah. This was a place that President Young had prepared for a resting place for the poor that could not prosecute the journey. It was a nice-looking place situated on Grand River (probably Soldier River now). Here I rented a log house for a short time, but did not feel satisfied. Here I found the heads of the Church had gone to the Missouri River. I wanted to get near to where the heads of the Church were, thinking I would get more information than I would back in the rear, and then I did not like Grand River for winter.

Accordingly, in a few days I took James W. Stewart with me [Cynthia's brother] and went on to the Missouri River. Here I found an uncle to my wife, William Stewart, with whom we stopped a day and then returned to Pisgah in time to be at the confinement of my wife on the twenty-second of August, 1846. My oldest son was born at Mt. Pisgah, then Pottawattamie County in the state of Iowa.

In about two weeks after this event I took the teams and went back to Kelsey's Mills after provisions I had bought and left there as we came out. I was gone between two and three weeks on this trip. When I returned, I found my wife and child well, as well as the rest of the family. During my absence, once of my neighbors had killed two of my cows, quite a loss to me as we were where I could not replace them. I brought him before Charles C. Rich, who was there to preside, but was told plainly that, as I did not belong to the Church, that my testimony could not be taken against one who did belong to the Church. This seemed rather hard for me to bear, as if I could not tell the truth before being baptized. Still, I passed over it as well as I could.

~AP~
CHAPTER 7

GEORGE WASHINGTON HILL
(5X) Great Grandpa
TRULY HARD TIMES

$$ MONEY PROBLEMS $

About the first of October we hitched up and rolled out for the Missouri River and selected a place for wintering on the Booyou River (probably the Boyer River) [in Harrison Co, Iowa, north of Council Bluffs] on account of the joint rushes that grew there in abundance and kept green all winter; stock do well on joint rushes. Here I had my last cow stolen and had one mare and colt drowned in the Booyou River.

Here we had a very hard winter and were very poorly prepared for it; we had a very hard time. I built a small log house with a chimney, made of sods cut out with a spade. We were very poorly clad, poorly fed, poorly housed, and I think the most severe winter I ever experienced. It seemed as if the adversary was determined to leave no stone unturned that would discourage me or that would hinder me in the prosecution of the journey or the accomplishing of the purpose for which I had set out, but I had endeavored to count the cost before starting and I had determined to go through if I had to go alone and on foot with nothing, realizing that the Savior's words were just as true when he said, "He that will not leave father and mother, houses and lands, wives and children, is not worthy of me," as when He said, "He that believeth and is baptized shall be saved." So that the exertions of the adversary were all wasted on me; they never served to discourage me in the least. They had but one effect on me, and that was to make me weep when alone that circumstances were so hard with me that I could not provide any better for those who were dependent on me during this winter.

We had a good many councils as to how we should provide for the journey in the spring. We had neither money nor teams and provisions sufficient for the journey, and how to obtain them was the great consideration with us. My wife's mother had an old Negro woman slave. She wanted the boys, some of them, to take off to Missouri and sell her, as she had become dissatisfied and did not want to go any farther, but they refused. I should do this job.

Finally I consented to take her and do the best I could with her, so I got one of the boys to go with me as far as Council Point where I sold her to Captain Whitehead for fifty dollars in cash, two yoke of cattle and one wagon. The wagon, oxen and cows I had to go to Missouri after. I sent every cent of the money home with the boy that went with me lest I should be obliged to spend some of it for something to eat. And away I went after the cows and oxen, and this was a severe job, as I had two cows to drive loose and the oxen and wagon, this giving me plenty of exercise. In fact, it kept me running nearly all the time. The snow was pretty deep and the wind came howling down the Missouri Bottoms, driving the snow in my face for four of the coldest successive days that I had ever experienced.

I finally arrived home with my cows, oxen and wagon without injury except that I had frozen my ears, but I thought I got off well at that. My wife's mother was well pleased with what I had done and promised me one of the cows, but I never realized the promise. We remained in this place until the middle of February when I concluded to move over into Winter Quarters and get to work preparing the journey the following summer. We were now busy fitting up the pioneers.

I now tried to get my oldest brother-in-law to remain and bring on his mother and brothers and sisters and let me go with the pioneers, but he absolutely refused. He said he would have nothing to do with bringing that great family of children into the wilderness to starve to death, but offered to go with the pioneers himself if I would remain and bring on the family. To this I finally gave my consent and went to work and fitted my own team and wagon. In company with my wife's uncle, William Stewart, we got our team and outfit fitted up according to requirements and started them off with the pioneers about the middle of April, 1847.

I now turned my attention to getting ready for following with the families. This involved another trip to Missouri, a distance of one hundred and twenty-five miles and back, making some two hundred and fifty miles. With ox teams that had to travel over one thousand miles with heavy loads and without roads to travel on, there was only one thing that made the venture [seems to be a word left out of this sentence somewhere] to start from the Missouri River in 1847, and that was the health of my wife.

She had taken the scurvy in the winter, superinduced [sic] by our living as we did without vegetables. And as soon as the weather began to get warmer in the spring, she got worse instead of better and came very near dying. In fact, I had no hopes for her but to get on the road traveling as soon as possible, thinking a change of scenery, a change of air, and a change of water might be beneficial to her. I was determined to try it, let the consequences be what they might. I knew that we did not have money enough to get a decent outfit to go with, but I would have preferred to have started with my gun only and to have taken my chance as an Indian rather than to have remained in that inhospitable region with the scurvy taking the people off by the hundreds as it was doing.

Accordingly, I took what money we had, and taking G. R. Stewart [Ruthy's second son] with me to drive one of the teams, away we went to Missouri to get an outfit which consisted of three hundred and fifty pounds of corn to each one in the family. This was to do us some eighteen months and would leave us at least one thousand miles from where we could procure fresh supplies in case we did not raise anything the next year. You may think this a very hazardous undertaking. Well, we thought so too, but the stakes were terrible we had to play.

Shortly after my return, I was baptized by Benjamin S. Clapp at Winter Quarters, now Florence. This was in the forepart of June. We now hastened our departure from Winter Quarters, glad to get from that inhospitable place with life even, for we did not think we should have had even that if we had remained much longer. We made our way as best we could to the Elkhorn River to the place where we would be organized for the journey. Here we had to make a raft of logs to ferry over the river. I assisted to ferry the whole of the companies, consisting of some five hundred and sixty wagons, over this river on a log raft, accomplishing this feat without accident of any note. We were here organized into A. O. Smoot's hundred, Major Russell's fifty and Samuel Turnbow's 10. We had got fairly started on the journey.

It was amusing to see us with our oxen, cows and two-year olds all yoked up, and in some instances the yearlings, as we thought that even yearlings could pull something, following the tracks the pioneers had made through the illimitable prairie, going we knew not where, but determined to seek an asylum where Christian charity would never come, notwithstanding our destitute condition. We left, indeed, without a regret. For some five hundred miles we traveled in one body as much as possible for protection against Indians that swarmed in thousands over the plains.

As soon as we had got fairly under way, I was appointed hunter for the company. This increased my labors a great deal, for whenever we were in camp I was off with my gun trying to obtain meat for the fifty. And sometimes while traveling I would leave my wife, although she was hardly able to sit up, to drive the team of four yoke of cattle, and take my gun and travel for miles away from the track to procure meat. In this way I have killed deer and hung them on my shoulders and carried them for as much as four miles without laying them down. And always, as soon as camp was formed in the evening, in the place of resting myself from the labors of the day, I would take my gun and go and try for meat. In this way I managed to keep meat for the family all the way and for the company most of the time.

~AP~
CHAPTER 8

GEORGE WASHINGTON HILL
(5X) Great Grandpa

GULLY ROCKS & THE 3 BEARS

I well remember the day that I saw the first antelope and the first buffalo. We had just started when the wagon G. R. Stewart was driving broke and the company had to stop and put up the blacksmith shop to repair it. The captain came to see me and said we would not get started anymore that day and wanted me to go hunting. There were several that wanted to go, as we expected to go a good ways. It was decided that we should go horseback.

I rode a mule belonging to my wife's uncle, William Stewart. Well, when we had got a good ways out, we found an antelope, and some of the boys, having heard that to raise a red handkerchief that they would come to you, accordingly Albert Dewey pulled out his ramrod and tied his handkerchief on it and went riding around on the smooth prairie trying to coax the antelope up to him. In reality, if he had seen the antelope before it saw him and had secreted himself where the antelope could not have seen him, and then have hoisted something, the antelope might have come nigh enough to him to see what it was to enable him to have shot it, but as it was, his riding around on the smooth prairie in plain sight only made the antelope run so much faster away from him. But as he ran from Brother Dewey, he did not notice well enough where he was, for he came running by me at full speed within about one hundred and fifty yards of me. Now this was entirely too nigh me for an animal to attempt to pass me in safety.

I brought up my gun and knocked him down at once. Just at this time we saw two buffalo come over a hill some two miles away with General Charles C. Rich and Doctor Richardson in full chase after them.

So I hastened and reloaded my gun and left my antelope lying where he fell and joined in the chase after the buffalo, but my mule would not run worth a cent. I continued to urge him, and it seemed like the more I urged him the farther I got behind. We had taken up a small hollow, thinking to intercept the buffalo at the crossing of this hollow, as their course was quartering toward us. Well, in about one mile running, I was left one hundred yards behind.

I had begun to think that mules were not much on the run, but as the buffalo were crossing the hollow, the foremost of the horsemen were within about one hundred yards of them, and when the mule saw the buffalo come bounding down the hill, he became wonderfully excited. Now it was that he showed us what a mule could do at running, and although he fell so much behind while I was whipping and spurring him with all my might, when he saw the buffalo, he lit out at such a rate that I do not think we went more than two hundred yards until he brought me alongside the horses, jumping, it seemed to me, as high as my head every jump, and so stiff-legged that just as I was passing the first horseman, one stirrup broke.

This bothered me considerably, but just as I was nearing Doctor Richardson, he fired on the buffalo. His horse fetched a skip to one side and he lit flat on his back. Seeing the Doctor shoot and fall almost by his side excited him [the donkey] still more, and he jumped so furiously that my other stirrup strap broke. This almost unhorsed me, and seeing where my stirrup fell, I thought to stop and get it, but he carried me so far before I could get him stopped that I could not find it, so

I straddled him and joined the chase. But I had hindered so much time looking for the stirrup that they had both of the buffalo down before I got to them. The boys loaded their horses with meat of the buffalo, but I preferred antelope, so I went back to where I had killed the antelope and put him on my mule and started for camp. I also killed the largest and fattest badger that I almost ever saw and carried him to camp, thinking that he was good to eat. Now we had got so far from the camp that it was just midnight when we got to camp. This was my first day with buffalo and antelope and the first badger I had ever seen.

In about two or three more days' travel we got into buffalo country where we could see them by the thousands. We would now see them all around us as far as the eye could reach, as thick as you would generally see a cow herd. We had now to guard against their stampeding our stock.

We continued our journey in this way on the north side of the Platte River until we got opposite what is now called Ofalon's Bluffs on South Platte. Here Jedediah Grant's cattle got stampeded and he lost about sixty head. We stopped here for a few days trying to find his stock. I went over to South Platte in company with A. O. Smoot, Samuel Turnbow, George B. Wallace and Peter Nebeker, hunting for the stock belonging to Brother Grant's company. In running the buffalo along the South Platte, there was a buffalo cow who broke one of her forelegs in jumping down the bank. This crippled her, so that we concluded to drive her to camp and butcher her, but when we went into the river to drive her out she only drove at us.

We continued driving until she drove us clear across the river which was about two miles wide, but when she got to the bank she refused to go up, so we threw two lariats on her and undertook to pull her up, but she was too good at holding back. I then went into the river and took my butcher knife and would prod her in the rump, thinking to make her go up that way, but it was no go. Finally Brother Smoot took a bit of a run and jumped straddle of her, thinking to ride her up the bank, but she had kicked so when I was prodding her that she was just as wet as water would make her, which made her so slick he never made any stop on her, but landed head foremost in the river. But she concluded that she had rather go up the bank alone than to be ridden up, so up she went, charging.

The boys now spread apart with their lariats and held her while I came up the bank and got my gun and shot her as a beef. While we were dressing her, there came the most singular-looking animal that we had ever seen. Brother Smoot requested me to kill it. I took my gun and just as it came to river and commenced to drink, I shot him. When he dropped dead into the river, he sank like a rock, and with all the hunting we could do, we could not find him, so that we never knew what he was. He looked like a wolf with long, shaggy hair and was white, but what he was we never knew.

While some of the boys were dressing our buffalo, the rest of us were chasing the buffalo and found a steer that had been left by Oregon emigrants,

I suppose on account of lameness, as he was quite lame. But we drove him to camp with us and brought him to the valley with us, but we got none of the lost cattle. After searching for the stampeded stock until it was considered in vain to search longer, we continued our journey.

We arrived opposite Scott's Bluffs (now Scottsbluff) on Saturday night, and as we always laid by on Sunday to let our animals rest, some of us boys concluded to cross the river and ascend the bluffs. Accordingly, several of us went and ascended them to the top, finding some mountain sheep on the top of the bluffs. We chased them, thinking that we could make them jump off of the cliffs and kill themselves, but we found out that they could ascend or descend precipitous rocks better than we could. In fact, they would skip up and down cliffs that seemed to be almost perpendicular.

On coming down off of these bluffs, I heard a call from one of the members of our party who was hanging from the edge of a cliff. When descending this precipice, he had happened to look down, and seeing the distance so great below him, he became excited and had stuck his fingers in a crack of the rock and held on for dear life, continuing to look below him. He could not control his nerves, but was trembling like an aspen leaf when I got to him. And seeing the condition he was in, I took him in my arms and carried him by force to a place of safety, thus saving him from falling several hundred feet and dashing himself to pieces. I then remained with him until he arrived safely at the bottom of the bluffs.

We continued our journey on the north side of the river until we came to the mouth of Laramie, for here we crossed over on the south side near old Fort John, near where Fort Laramie now stands. About five miles above here at a grove of white ash, we camped and laid by for about a week to burn tar, there being plenty of pitch pine here. We also needed rest. From here we went on to Horse Shoe, about forty miles. Here we laid by one day for the women to wash.

We were now fairly well into the Black Hills and in full view of Laramie Peak. This was such a novel sight to me that I proposed to Captain Turnbow that we should go to the top of the peak and kill some mountain sheep which were supposed to abound there. He accepted the proposal and away we went, supposing it to be about ten or twelve miles, when in reality it was about forty miles. We went about twelve miles and the peak looked just as far off as it did [originally]. We got discouraged about going to it and returned the same day as we started.

Here we came across an old buffalo bull, and Turnbow proposed that I should crawl as close to him as I could and shoot him, and we would load ourselves with meat and return. So I crawled up within three rods of him, as he was feeding away from me, but he would not turn around so as to give me a fair shot at him. So I peeled away at his flank, ranging forward. At the crack of a gun, he jumped and kicked and ran; in a short distance he entered the brush out of sight. Turnbow came up laughing and we followed his track a little ways into the brush when I saw him walking along with his head down, very sick, so I shot him again. He ran off a very little ways and stopped and laid down, too sick to go farther.

Turnbow now proposed to shoot him in the ear, saying he had heard it said that a bullet would not penetrate a buffalo's head, and he was going to try it and see for himself. So he went up within about one rod of the old bull, as he was lying there with his tongue out, and raised his gun, when the old bull began to struggle to get up.

Turnbow thought he was gone sure. He jerked his hat and ran as hard as I ever saw a man run until he got to some cottonwood trees about forty yards off before he looked behind him, thinking the old bull was right at his heels, while I was laughing almost fit to split my sides to see him run, as there was no danger. The old bull hardly got to his feet when he fell dead, before Turnbow was half way to the trees. When he saw the old bull was dead, he came back laughing, saying he was going to have his shot anyhow. So he went about to where he was before and peeled away, the bullet going into his head just the same as any other beef.

We now went to work and skinned a part of him and cut off about one hundred and fifty pounds of the meat. I objected to taking so much, telling him he would give out and we would have to leave it after carrying it a good way, but he declared he knew he could carry it to camp. So we strung it on a pole between us and started for camp, but he soon got tired and we would have to lay it down and rest, then we would start on again with the whole of it in place of throwing a part of it away so as to make it light enough so that we could carry it.

In this way we continued carrying and resting until we got about half way to camp when he declared he could not carry it any farther. So he proposed we should hang it up in a tree and go to camp and come after it in the morning with horses. Finally I agreed, so I climbed a tree and hung it up and we went to camp.

That night the Indians stole every horse in camp but seven head. We knew it was folly to pursue them on foot, so we gave them up and proceeded on our journey. Having had experience enough the day before in carrying on foot, we left our meat to hang and dry and did not go for it, so that we had our tramp to Laramie for nothing.

In ths way we traveled until we had come out of the hills onto the Platte again. As we were coming along one evening just before camping time, we saw three bears on the other side of the river near by a thicket of brush. Smoot, the captain, called to me to get ready and go with him and kill them. Accordingly, I got my gun which was empty and loaded it with a double charge, as I knew it would stand it, and took my pistol–a single barrel–in case I got into a close fight, and went with him. By the time we got started, there were three more boys who had got ready and also went with us. Their names were Charles Chipman, George Peacock, and Lorin Roundy. Well, by the time we got across the river, the bears had gone into the brush so that we could not see them, but we had three large dogs with us which we put on their tracks and into the brush they ran, but when they got to the bears they were so astonished they would not even bark at them.

When we got pretty well up to the brush, Smoot charged right up, thinking, I suppose, to get the first shot, but when he saw the bear he was about like the dogs.

He was so excited he forgot he had any gun, but hollered, "Here she is boys, come and shoot her quick." Accordingly we ran as fast as we could right up to the brush, but when we got there the brush was high enough that we could not see them on foot. Just at this time the old bear noticed Smoot on his horse and she paid no attention to the dogs, but came for us with a vengeance. This excited Smoot the more, and he hollered, "Take care boys, run— here she comes. She is a fifteen-hundreder," and turning his horse he laid whip and away he went with a vengeance.

This so alarmed the boys that they all turned and ran as fast as they could, leaving the bear and me to settle our little differences as best we could. In the moment of their running by me and leaving me to fight it out alone, I thought of Daniel Boone's companions running and leaving him alone in like circumstances when attacked by a panther. But I thought I was equal to the emergency and knowing my gun and myself also, I brought my gun to my face and ran backwards from the brush to try and get far enough from the brush to give me a chance to shoot. The old bear, in the meantime was not fooling away her time, for I had not got more than twenty feet from the brush until she made her appearance.

When she saw me, she was filled with rage and she came for me with all the vengeance that she had in her, blowing and whistling so that you might have heard her a half mile at least. But there was no time to lose, so, quick as thought I brought my gun on her and fired, striking her in the sticking place and coming out through her kidney, knocking her a complete somersault with her head from me.

I immediately reloaded, turning the powder into my gun out of the powder horn while I was getting a bullet out of my mouth where I had placed them to be ready for a load quick, for I expected a fight. I had not started from camp after them [the bears] calculating to run from them when I saw them.

After I had killed this one, which proved to be an old she-grizzly with her teeth all worn off, I looked to see what had become of my companions. They were just turning around some large trees about fifty yards from me when they saw the bear down and that I was master of the field. They came running back as fast as they had run away, but I was reloaded and ready for another before they got back to me.

We then got the dogs after the young ones; the dogs would fight these. They all three turned loose on one bear, but they could not stop him. He would travel along as fast as a man could walk with all three dogs doing their best on him. I went up to him while the dogs and he were fighting and ran my knife through him, killing him instantly.

The other one fled and got across the river and almost the whole company ran after him. Of all the dogs in camp there was but one that would fight him, and he could not do much with him. Then a man by the name of Armstrong got to him and putting his gun close to the bear's head, he fired, missing him. He then turned the butt of his gun and struck the bear over the head, breaking the gun into two pieces, but not hurting the bear any. This brought him to his senses.

There was another fellow that ran up to the bear and did the same way and missed him. Not taking time to bring any ammunition with them, and not having any more guns, they had no other resource but to throw rocks at it. Finally Major Russell, the captain of the fifty, hit him on the nose with a rock and knocked him down and he laid there until he ran up and cut his throat. Thus ended the first bear fight I was ever in.

~AP~
CHAPTER 9

GEORGE WASHINGTON HILL
(5X) Great Grandpa

POUR, HUNGRY & NAKED ALIKE!

We now proceeded slowly. Our teams were getting worn out with heavy loads and no roads. We traveled slowly until we got to the Pacific Springs. Here we met the First Presidency returning from Salt Lake Valley. Here our hearts were made glad by their rehearsing to us that they had found a good country at Salt Lake Valley, counseled us on our arrival in Salt Lake Valley to weigh out our provisions and ration ourselves so as to make it hold out until time for harvest.

From here to Fort Bridger, game was scarce; but little could be got while traveling. At the Springs, six miles west of Bridger, I left the wagons and went on foot alone to Bear River to try and kill some meat to do us into the valley. I made Bear River a little after dark, and the next morning started on a hunt in the hills, hoping to kill several antelope that day, as I expected the wagons to get there that night. I soon had a very fat antelope down and another large buck came running up to see what the noise was. I blazed away at him, thinking I had him sure, but the tube and cylinder blew out of my gun and I do not suppose the bullet went half way to him. My hunt was now played out. After my leaving my wife two days, I got but one antelope. Still, I thought it would never do to give it up, so I took another gun to try it the next day while the train was on the move.

I started out in the morning, but I had not gone more than two or three miles before I came on a mule and mare that had been left there by the Battalion boys a couple of months before. [These must have been some of the sick from the Battalion who wintered in Pueblo and then came on to SL Valley about the same time as Brigham Young and the first pioneers. Wonder how he knew they belonged to the Battalion?] They were as wild as if they had never seen anybody in their lives. I tried a good while to get the better of them, to catch them, but finding my efforts unavailing, I undertook to graze the mare, thinking by so doing I should get them both. So I blazed away and down came the mare. I ran up to her and slipped a bridle on her, taking the bridle off the horse I was riding and letting it go on the prairie. The one I rode ran off with the wild mule. I gave the bridle to Brother Chipman who was with me to hold, telling him to get something and stop up the bullet hole so as to stop up the blood while I went after the one that had run away. It took me a good while to catch my horse. I was gone over an hour. In the meantime, Chipman thought the mare bled so fast that she would bleed to death anyhow, so he took the bridle off her and turned her loose. She got up and went off down by the train just as I was getting back and fell down dead. I then gave up the mule and came ahead.

When we got over into Echo Canyon, we met James W. Stewart with my oxen that I had sent out with the pioneers, to help us over the mountains. This was timely help, and it enabled us to cross the mountains a great deal easier than we could otherwise have done.

In East Canyon I came very near having an accident that would have been quite serious. My oxen refused to take a crossing straight. They crowded me into the haw side and ran the wagon up on the bank so far they came very near upsetting my wagon. I was obliged to turn around to the off side and take the wagon on my back and hold it until we could drive down into the creek. My wagon was loaded with provisions which, if it had tipped over into the creek, would almost have ruined us, but we got over safely and arrived where Salt Lake City now stands, on the eighteenth day of September, 1847.

We had now got to our journey's end. As soon as we could after we had got to our camping ground so that we could do it, we went to work and weighed out our provisions. We found that we had a little over three-fourths of a pound of corn a day to the head.

Having accomplished all I had agreed to do, and that was to see my wife's mother to her journey's end in safety, we now separated and each went to ourselves. It had occupied my time and had caused me a great deal of hard work in taking the responsibility of her family and bringing them through, but once having given my word, I was determined to accomplish it and although I was as tough as men ever get to be, I was well-nigh worn out. In fact, I had been judged to be forty-five years old before I got to the valley, although I was but twenty-five.

I now went to work and got out logs and built a log house in the fort and prepared for the winter. During this winter, the Indians stole a great deal of our stock. They got the last I had, which set me entirely afoot. Neither was there any chance to get a new supply for work. We were all poor together. The first winter was very light; in fact, there was ploughing and sowing done all winter. In the spring of 1848, I went out on Mill Creek six miles south. Here I managed to get in about ten acres of corn, but just as my corn was up nicely, the crickets came down in swarms from the mountains and in one day's time destroyed my whole crop, and where they ate it never grew again. They would suck all the virtue out of the roots. I then took ten acres to attend on shares, but the nights were so cold that it would not grow worth a cent and there was not any that ripened fit to eat. Still, we had to eat it, soft, mushy, half-rotten as it was. In the fall, I got to work for Van Vott and got about twenty bushels off him, but it was all of a piece —no sound corn in it. In fact, I almost came to the conclusion that we would have to import our seed corn. It seemed that we never could get any ripe enough for seed. It rained but very little, not enough to spoil the salt in the Lake, so but what it [the salt?] could be got all winter, but to say that we passed the first two years in destitute circumstances does not express the situation. But I believe today that notwithstanding we had to suffer so much for even the commonest necessities of life, that the first immigration [settlers] were the best satisfied and grumbled the least of any immigrants that have ever come to Utah.

We were all poor alike, **we were all hungry alike, and we were all naked alike** and we could each sympathize with each other.

Well, in this condition we passed the first years in the valley, the spring of forty-nine being the hardest I ever experienced. After we had eaten all the flour and corn meal and shorts that could be got, we would sift the bran through a sieve and eat it, and when we could get no more to sift, we would eat the siftings, and after all this, I passed some six weeks without the taste of bread of any kind and worked hard every day. In fact, one day I walked twenty-five miles and cut and split and ricked up with the hearts all to the sun, one hundred and fifty fence rails, twelve feet long and all of a large size, for twenty pounds of shorts, for Jacob Gates, and then when I went for my shorts he only gave me seventeen pounds.

Well, in this way we passed along and although I had money in my pocket, it would not buy bread. I remember just as harvest was coming on, my wife went to a meeting after a very scanty breakfast one Sunday morning, leaving absolutely nothing at home to eat. On our return she was so faint she wanted to go home at noon but I said no, I wanted to stay till the afternoon meeting and then I would get something to eat. So we stayed. After meeting she went home alone and I went to an emigrant camp that was camped up by the Hot Springs and bought some flour and coffee and away I went trudging home feeling larger than if I should have done if my load had been of gold. My wife went to work and cooked some pancakes and made a cup of coffee, but she was so weak that she could not eat but very little, but from this time we had plenty.

Now we began to realize he fulfillment of a prophecy of Heber C. Kimball's made the fall before. When President Young and Brother Kimball and others arrived with our second emigration, the people were in a very destitute condition. Heber came out on the stand and prophesied in the name of Israel's God that in less than twelve months everything we needed in the provision, grocery and dry goods line should be bought in the streets of Salt Lake cheaper than it would cost in St. Louis. He said himself, afterwards, he was scared for he did not know how such a prophecy could be fulfilled, but said that he said it before he knew what he was saying.

But it was now being fulfilled, for the emigrants came flocking in by thousands, loaded so heavy they did not know, but now they were in a hurry to get to the gold mines before the gold was all got, and they would pay fabulous prices for ponies and would sell anything they could for just what they could get. In some instances they would give a new wagon and three or four yoke of cattle and outfit for a pony that one month before could have been had for twenty-five dollars. It was just as Heber said it would be—ready-made clothing, calicos, domestics, flour, bacon, powder, lead and almost everything that we wanted, sold at less than St. Louis' prices. And then they brought the money along for us to buy their goods and gave it to us for a few ponies, a little garden sauce, butter and milk, and so on, so that by the time the emigration was over, the majority of the people were quite comfortable and Heber's prophecy had been fulfilled to the fullest extent.

~AP~
CHAPTER 10

GEORGE WASHINGTON HILL
(5X) Great Grandpa

WHEN YOU ARE OUTNUMBERED-

In September, 1849, I received a letter from father and brothers in Missouri of a tone that made me believe that if I were to go back that fall I should be able to bring them into the Church. I went to see President Young and told him what news I had from home and asked him what he thought I had better do. He counseled me to go back with a company of missionaries that would be going immediately after conference, so I set to work to get ready to go, the family of my wife's mother proffering me one-third of their estate that was left if I would get the remainder and bring it to them. This of itself was no consideration, as the whole amount was only about sixteen hundred dollars, but considering the prospects of getting my father's family out, I concluded to make the venture.

Accordingly, I moved my family up to Weber River to my wife's mother's and hired them to take care of them until my return, furnishing them nearly as much provisions as they used and paying G. R. Stewart one yoke of cattle on my return, besides cutting ten acres of wheat for them. October the tenth was the day appointed to start. On the ninth at sunset I started from Weber with a pack on my back of about thirty pounds to walk to Session's settlement [present-day Bountiful], a distance of thirty miles. Arriving at Session's settlement in the latter part of the night, I crawled into the wagon we were going in and slept rather than to disturb them at night.

The next day we started, but the rest of the company did not start until the fifteenth. We went to Fort Bridger and waited for the company of missionaries to come, when we proceeded on our journey from this point. I stood guard every night, the night being divided into three watches, standing my own guard, Kinkade's and Elder Taylor's. I walked all the way. I do not suppose I rode five miles the whole distance from Salt Lake to the Missouri River, and cooked for the mess and gained about fifteen pounds on the road. Just beyond Sweet Water River we met the mail. They had been robbed by the Crow Indians three times the day before, the last time the Indians taking everything they had, even making them strip off their shirts and exchange with them.

We divided with them what we could in clothing and provisions and sent them on their way rejoicing. These Crows, five hundred strong, were down on a war party to fight the Sioux. Finding the Sioux were too strong for them, they sent home for five hundred more men and were waiting for their arrival to go on to meet the Sioux.

When we got down to Platte River Canyon, we stopped at noon at the lower end of the canyon. Just as we were sitting down to dinner, the Cheyennes, about 200 strong, made a charge on us. Jedediah Grant, who was sergeant of the guard, instantly took command. Dinner was left on the ground; every man ran to arms. The horses were brought in and tied up and a line formed before the Indians got to us.

The Indians evidently intended to run right over us; they were well mounted and armed, their guns cocked. Those that had bows had their hands full of arrows. Several had swords; they were drawn. They came on in splendid style, about twelve abreast, and made about as handsome a sight as one would wish to look at. Still, one does not see a more dangerous sight often in a lifetime. Every man made his horse do his best, for they saw our movements and they knew that if we beat them into position, it was going to make it costly to them, if they succeeded at all in robbing us and getting our boxes and goods.

They came on at full speed until they were within about two or three rods of our line. Every man's gun was to his face.

When so many hollow things were looking them square in the face and no signs of any faltering by the holders of them, it was more than they could stand, and they stopped then and there. In fact, the stop was so sudden and unlooked for by them in the next lines that they piled up there in the worst confused mass you ever saw, some twenty or thirty being thrown from their horses.

A good many came very near being run over and they got into a regular quarrel amongst themselves. They made three attempts to pass around our lines, but were met every time with arms presented, when they finally desisted.

Finally, after being kept in this position by them for an hour or two, Jedediah called for five of the smallest to retire from the lines and harness up all the teams and put everything in the wagons, ready for a start. When this was done, he called for every teamster to go to his team and start out, and as the first team passed the line, for three men to fall in by the side of the team with arms on the shoulder and march by the side of the team, and to do the same throughout.

We did so, and when the Indians saw our move, about one half of them turned about and left as mad as they could well be. The rest went along with us quite a distance, to all appearances really friendly. That night we camped on Horse Shoe, close by the side of the Sioux camp, about one thousand strong. These and the Cheyennes, about two thousand, were both coming to fight the Crows. The Crows came about midnight and stole some ten head of their horses and about twenty head from the Cheyennes. Just as soon as it was daylight there was a perfect roar of small arms, every Indian discharging his gun to load afresh for the fight which came off that day back in the hills. The Crows took ths method of stealing their horses to draw the Sioux and Cheyennes into the ground where they wanted to fight, where they had an ambush laid for them.

We traveled that day down below the Fort Laramie kilns and camped with two Government teamsters. We saw that we were going to be short of provisions before we got through, so we inquired of these teamsters what the chance would be for us to get supplies at the fort. They said that there was plenty there that the Government had sent out on purpose for destitute emigrants, but assured us we could not get anything for they had known a good many to apply for them but were invariably refused. We told them that we would get all we wanted in answer to prayer. They said that if we did, they would become Mormons. Accordingly, when prayer time came, the chaplain was requested to say our condition before Father and ask him to soften the heart of the Major commanding so that he would supply our wants. The chaplain did so. After prayer, they said that they had never seen anything done that way, but if our prayers were answered, they would be Mormons.

The next day when we arrived at the fort, we called on the Major and made our wants known to him. His reply was, "Yes, gentlemen, you can have all you want at the wholesale price, at Fort Leavenworth prices, without anything for freight even." So we got everything we needed in answer to our prayers, but I have never seen the teamsters since I saw them at the fort. They kept watch to see if we got everything, swearing that it beat their time, but that was all there was of them.

The first night below Laramie it rained all night, making it bad traveling, but when we went to cross over from Ash Hollow, we found it had snowed there some ten or twelve inches deep and froze so hard that it would almost bear up the horses and mules, giving us a very hard day. But when we got to South Platte, there was no ice in the river, which was very low, but the sand was so soft that when we had gone about one fourth of a mile into the river, our teams all gave out and we were obliged to get out and push at the wagons before the teams could start again. We divided up and took one third of them at a time and helped them across and then returned for one more third. Here we had to make three round trips in the river, about knee deep, which took us over an hour in ice-cold water. Elder John Taylor had crossed on horseback and made up a rousing fire on the bank out of buffalo chips, as that was all the wood he had. But we never stopped to try to warm, but took to our heels and ran four or five miles to where we camped.

The snow met us at Plum Creek about three hundred miles from the Missouri River. From here on, we had snow about two feet deep, but fortune favored us again, for the wind had blown the snow all out of the road. But we had to chop cottonwood trees from nearly all the way for our horses to feed on the bark, as the snow was so deep they could get no grass. At Fort Carney they furnished us what we wanted.

We arrived at the Missouri River on December the twelfth, driving forty miles that day without breakfast. Here we found the ice running so thick that boats could not cross, so we laid by one day, held a meeting, and voted to cross the next day, on Monday, and I was appointed one of a committee to go up and find the best place. We crossed at the ferry on a strip of ice not over one hundred yards wide, in the current, with our horses and wagons where it was open water twenty-four hours before. We pulled our wagons with ropes, and when the wagon wheels would cut through the ice, as many did, I would step up and take hold of the point of the hub and lift it out and the rest of the boys would pull it along. We got two horses into the river, but we would choke them and make them rise and pull them out and go on. We had been over the river about one hour when the river cleared itself of ice, but we were over as we voted we would be, on the bridge that Father prepared for us.

Now we made our way to Kanesville [Iowa] where I tarried one week with the brethren before starting on. I bade the brethren goodbye and started on foot and alone for southwest Missouri, about 500 miles, where I arrived between Christmas and New Year's, finding my folks all well except my father who was barely able to get about. All were overjoyed to see me, but father had had a severe attack of congestive chills the April previous and had never got over it.

Indeed, it seemed that he had just lived to see me before he could die. Early in February, he appointed the following Sunday for me to baptize him, he being the first one that called for baptism, but on Saturday night he was violently attacked with fever from which he never recovered, and died on the following Saturday night, full in the faith without the privilege of baptism.

I now prosecuted my suit in court for the money I had come after; this caused me a great deal of traveling. I went once to Jefferson City to meet Joseph Toronto, who was going to Italy on a mission with Elder Lorenzo Snow. But, I accomplished all I went for: I got my money all right, baptized my oldest brother and family also. We spent the most of the winter traveling and as soon as spring opened, were ready for a start from Florence, Nebraska.

~AP~
CHAPTER 11

GEORGE WASHINGTON HILL
(5X) Great Grandpa

BRIBES-PROMISES-DREAMS

-A dream, courtroom surprises, & promises

On my return trip, I had found that all my old acquaintances had turned enemies to me because of their suspicions that I had got to be a Mormon, for I had not told any of them that I had joined the Church. There is one incident I will relate.

On my way to court, I stayed overnight with a man by the name of Noah Bray, my brother Richard being with me. That night I dreamed that the opposition was very strong against me, that one J.A.J. Lee, one of the judges, had offered to bribe the court for one hundred dollars so that I need have no more expenses. In consequence of my refusing to bribe him, he had turned enemy to me and was trying to do all he could against me. I dreamed just what to do and also what would take place in the court room the next day.

In the morning when I got up, I told Bray he had got to go to court that day as he was one of the judges, but he not being on that term of the court and fixing to get off to California, but I told him if he did not I should send after him, for I was going to rule some of the judges off of the bench and was going to put him in their place. He said I could not do it; I told him I could. I then told him what I had seen the night before and that I was going to be governed by it that day to the letter.

So he went with us and everything transpired just exactly as I told him before we started. Even old Mike Randleman, the blacksmith, I dreamed, came into the court room at the ead of a mob with his sleeves rolled up to his shoulders and pinned up, and that when he came, that I stepped back into the jury room and adjusted my revolver and came out, and then they left.

Well, old Mike came just as I had seen him and stepped past the clerk and picked up a large green persimmon club that stood in the corner. I immediately stepped back and adjusted my revolver, and just as I was returning, the clerk took the club from old Mike and showed it to the Court, told them the Court House had been broken open a few nights before and that club was left, told Mike that that was his club and that Mike could not have it. The crowd then began to disperse and everything was done just as I had seen it the night before. This beat Noah Bray's time and he acknowledged that it beat anything he had ever seen.

I stopped one night at Harden Payne's where I believe there was an attempt made to poison me, when something said plainly to me not to eat supper. Well, I was so used to this thing that I took the warning and refused to eat after the victuals were on the table and the coffee was poured out. Whereupon the old lady got up from the table and took the cup of coffee that was poured out at my place and threw it out doors before my face. This entirely convinced me that I was right and that the monitor had given me timely warning.

Well, as soon as spring opened up [1850], we started. Nothing of an unusual occurrence took place until we got to Fort Carney. The cholera had set in a day or two back at Big Blue, but when we got to Platte River, the cholera had increased so much that my folks began to get frightened, when before I knew what I was saying, I told them not to be afraid of the cholera, that if they would do as I told them, they should pass through it and not have a symptom of it in my camp. This they agreed to do in a moment.

It was now my turn to get scared. I made the promise without knowing what I did. I now had to center all the faith I had in the Almighty. I knew he was able to keep us out of disease if we were faithful, and having made the promise without knowing how I came to do it, I knew I was under the influence of the Spirit or I never would dared to have made such a promise, no more than a sectarian preacher dare to promise the Holy Ghost, for he knows he has no authority to do so. So I took it that Father wanted to show his power, that they might receive strength, for they were very weak.

So we came right along for over three hundred miles where they were sick and dying around us all the time without one of my company having even a bowel complaint.

When we got to the old California crossing of South Platte, it was very high. Teams were swimming. I told the captain I would not cross there, that I could find a crossing just a little above where we could cross dry. So I took his horse and found a crossing where the water did not touch the wagon box. I then piloted them all over, crossing the river nine times that day, but when I had got the company all over without accident or getting anything wet, the captain called upon the company to furnish some teams and drivers to go back and bring my two wagons across at one trip, but notwithstanding I had been the means of their all crossing in safety without one man or woman even getting their feet wet, they all, without exception, refused to cross that river again to assist me to get across. I thanked them very kindly and told them that in my greatest extremity I could not accept of the assistance of any such a company; neither could I afford to travel with them any farther, and that they could find their own way the rest of the journey and I should help myself.

I had ferried the whole company over the Big Blue, working the whole day on the raft, as there was not a man in the whole company that had ever seen a wagon on a raft and knew no more about steering a raft than a new-born babe, and had rendered them the assistance that I had that day, and not one in the whole company had had the manhood to return the compliment even to make one trip to assist me. I got well nigh out of patience with them, but the captain declared he was ashamed of such ingratitude and took his teams, contrary to my wish, and went back with me after my wagons and brought me over safely at one trip. We then drove out to the spring and camped.

The next day we drove to Ash Hollow. The next morning I got up my teams early before the company was ready and bade them goodbye and rolled out of their company for good.

I then made the best of my way for home, but at Independence Rock my youngest brother took the mountain fever. Here we laid for eight days, during which time there came a man by the name of Brown that had a difficulty in his company and had got turned out of his company. He wanted to get to drive team from there to Salt Lake for his board, so I took him in and let him drive my team and left the wagons in care of my eldest brother and started from there alone on horseback to come on home in order to get in, if possible, before the celebration of the 24th.

At the head of Sweetwater I fell in with Charles Decker and Ralph Frink who had gone back in the same company the fall before. We were mutually glad to meet each other—me because I was entirely alone and they because they did not have a mouthful of anything to eat. Well, I divided grub with them, and by the time we reached Green River my grub was all gone. Here I bought what grub I thought would do us home, but when we reached Echo Canyon our grub was out again. Here we ate the last we had, about half a breakfast, and started for Salt Lake.

I found the Weber River pretty high, sometimes swimming my horse. I undertook to go over the point of mountain to avoid a very bad crossing. Here my mare fell and rolled down the mountain about fifty yards and lodged with her back under a log that was fast at the roots and her heels up the mountain in such a way that I could not extricate her, and I was obliged to chop the log in two with my butcher knife, as I had nothing else. This hindered a good deal of time and when I got her at liberty, I found that she was seriously injured. However, I started on, but at the next crossing the river had enlarged its channel when high and filled in next the bank with quicksand, and as soon as my mare struck this she mired up to her belly the first plunge she made, and every exertion she made afterwards still sank her deeper into the mire. Here I labored until nearly sunset trying to extricate her, but to no avail, for every move I made to get her out only sank her deeper in the mire. So I finally gave her up and started on foot with a heavy pack on my back.

I went on until dark, turned in by the side of a large rock, and slept until morning. But it was so very brushy in the canyon—no trail—the brush in many places so very thick it seemed almost impossible to get through, so I thought I would try the mountain, knowing that Weber and Ogden Rivers were not far apart where they came into the valley.

I thought the top of the mountain would be smooth and clear of brush, so up I went, toiling until I got near the top, when to my surprise, I found it was only a succession of mountains and canyons and altogether impracticable to follow the top of the mountains, and also I could see down into Weber Valley, a nice open country, clear of brush, and that I was almost to it when I ascended the mountain. So I retraced my steps, taking me about half a day to get to the top of the mountain and down again, and gaining not more than 3 or 4 miles.

I now struck out in earnest, but about noon there came a tremendous rain that hindered me for a couple of hours or more so that night overtook me again up in the head of Weber Canyon, above Devil's Gate. Here I laid down and slept by the side of a rock again. As soon as daylight came, I started on and reached home about noon, making the third day without anything to eat and two days with a pack upon my back that would weight close to one hundred pounds, especially after the rain the second day.

I found my family that I had not heard from since I left them in the previous October all well and very glad to see me, for they had heard how the cholera had raged on the plains and had been very uneasy about me. I had accomplished all I went to do, just as President Young told me I would, for I had obtained the means I went after and had succeeded in bringing my father's family into the Church—all but my brother John—and had brought them home with me, and although the cholera raged so fiercely on the plains, we all came through it without one of my company having a symptom of it, my promise being fulfilled to the very letter.

I have always believed that the angels of God accompanied me across the plains and guarded me from accidents and disease, and when I was coming down Weber Canyon alone with my pack on my back, every once in a while there would come the most cheerful influence over me and I do not know how many times I caught myself turning around to speak to my companion when I knew that I was entirely alone. Neither in the whole three days did I ever once feel the pangs of hunger nor fatigue, and my strength kept up seemingly as good as ever.

There is one singular circumstance that took place that I will here relate. We had a man with us by the name of Benton that, stop where we would, he would go fishing and he would scarcely ever fail to catch a mess of fish. If it was only a brook, he would have fish. Anyhow, while on Little Blue he caught a fine string of very large, fine fish, and when I saw them it seemed to me I never wanted anything so bad in my life, so I tried every way possible to get one of them, but he absolutely refused to let me have even one of them. After laboring with him for a good while to no purpose, offering him any price he had a mind to ask, I seemed to become angered at him and spoke right out to him and told him if he did not let me have one at least of his fish, he should not catch another fish for three hundred miles.

This seemed to enrage him and he asked if there were no fish in Platte River. I told him "yes," but he should not catch one in Platte River nor any of its tributaries. "Well," said he, "you shall not have one now at any price," and I was not able to buy one of them. "But," said he, "when we get over to Platte River, I will go and catch a mess and give them to you," at which I replied, "If you catch a fish in Platte River or any of its tributaries, you can call me a liar," and we parted.

Well, when we got over to Platte, he went fishing as usual, but got no bites. The next day he did the same with the same results. In a few days he took the cholera, but as soon as he was better enough he went fishing again. He continued this without a bite until I left them.

Well, as I was leaving my wagons on Sweetwater to come home, who should I meet but Benton. Said he as soon as the first salutations were over, "Mister Hill, are there any fish in this river?" I told him there were plenty. Said he, "I wish you would let me go and catch a mess, for I never was so hungry for fish in my life." I asked him if he caught any in the Black Hills. He said no, that he could see them in Deer Creek almost as thick as they could swim, but the moment he would throw in his hook, they would every one run away as fast as they could, and he had not had a bite of fish since we were at Little Blue, and he never was so hungry for fish in his life, and he would be very much obliged if I would allow him to go catch some.

At the same time he declared that if he were ever allowed to catch fish again as he used to, he would never refuse a man fish as he had me. I told him that he might go in the morning and catch what he wanted for all of me, for I should not hinder him. He seemed to be delighted, but I never saw him afterwards, so I do not know whether he got any in the morning or not, but in all our travels until this occurrence took place, we would never stop at any little branch or creek of any size, even where you would think there would not be even a minnow hardly, but what he would go and catch a good mess of fish. Still, in all that distance he never got a bite, just as I told him he should not.

Having arrived at home where I could rest and recruit myself again after a long and hazardous journey, I remained as quiet as circumstances would admit of. I now cast about to see where I should locate. Finally I selected a location about one mile south of the present site of Ogden City, had a tract of land surveyed of 53 acres, and went to work to build upon it. While engaged in building, there was an event transpired common in new countries, thickly peopled as this was with wild Indians.

There was an Indian chief named Tar-Ra-Kee that had made a practice of stealing corn from a man named Urban Stewart. One day Tar-ra-kee was in Urban's house and Urban told him that if he stole any more of his corn he would kill him. He said he was going to move away the next day. Well, about midnight that same night here comes Tar-ra-kee to steal more corn.

I suppose he wanted some to take along with him. Urban heard him shucking his corn, so he got up, took his gun and went out and shot him, sure enough killing him right there. It was now time for Urban to get scared, so he took his children and ran the best he could and came right over to my mother-in-law's house for safety. The Indians gathered up immediately and started on the warpath. Coming across three men going out after stock, they gave chase. Two made good their escape, but one by the name of Campbell was overtaken and killed. In the meantime, Little Soldier took Urban's track and followed him direct to our house where he was secreted, but we told him we knew nothing of him. Still he was not satisfied. However, he gave us until nine o'clock next day to get him and give him up.

It was now getting time for us to take the warpath, so we sent to Salt Lake for men and when the Indians came in the morning to see if we were going to give up Urban, they found over one hundred men there waiting for them. So [we] promptly took them prisoners and started after the others that had fled after killing Campbell. We followed them about twenty-five miles when we found they had scattered in every direction, so we returned. They were still not satisfied, for early in the spring they commenced stealing our horses and cattle, so we took the warpath again and followed them some fifty miles, catching up with their camp, but they had taken to the mountains. We caught one, however, and killed him and recovered a portion of the horses they had stolen.

We followed this up by another campaign of ten days, but they had run far enough that we did not overtake them, but they now gave it up and peace was restored again.

Things continued in this way until the spring of 1855, when at the April conference I was called to take a mission to the House of Israel [Indians]. This took all I could do to raise an outfit for myself, but realizing that the call was from God, I accepted it in good faith and went to work with a will to prepare for it. This took everything I could raise to fit myself out and a very poor outfit it was that I had. Still, I made the best I could of it and started early in May.

This mission lasted for three years. There were many things transpired upon that mission that are worthy of note, but I shall only mention a few of them.

None of us knew the language of the people we were sent to. Since I had learned a little of the language the winter before, it fell to my lot to do all the talking pretty much that was done, and also I had accepted the mission in good faith and did not want to return with a blank record, so I turned in with a will to try and get the language, realizing that unless I could talk with them, my labors would not amount to much.

I had faith in God that he would assist me if I would do my duty on my part. This I determined to do and it had been sealed upon my head that I should see them in the distance and should know them and that they would come to me by the hundreds, but little did I think that this was going to come literally to pass as soon as it did, for the first Indians we saw were at Fort Hall on Snake river. I went right to work on my missionary labors.

We were encamped on the Portneuf River about five miles from the fort. We had just encamped when, on looking over to Fort Hall, I discovered some Indians coming directly towards us, when it seemed to me that I knew them, and I told the boys who were with me that there came some of my children and that I was going to baptize them. This created some merriment among the boys, but on they came, arriving at our camp. They got off their horses and shook hands with us and stopped with us, when I went to talking to them as well as I could, telling them who we were and what our business was.

The next day we moved on up the ferry, the Indians accompanying us, when on coming into camp the President called upon me to preach to them, which I did as well as I could which was very poor indeed. When they called for baptism, I took them to the river and baptized them, in fulfillment of my prediction that I had made when I first saw them in the distance. This was my first Indian baptism.

~AP~

CHAPTER 12

GEORGE WASHINGTON HILL
(5X) Great Grandpa

GONE FISHING

(A deadly sport)

We then proceeded on our journey to the Salmon River where we made a location. As we were going from Snake to Salmon River, we met the Bannock Chief and he accompanied us to our destination and stopped with us until the fishing season was over when he went on his accustomed buffalo hunt.

As we approached the Salmon River, the chief and myself made a treaty between ourselves, each agreeing what we would do to preserve peace and friendship between us, the chief telling me that Father, meaning the Great Spirit, had told him that the white men were coming to his country and he must meet them and welcome them to his country, and he must hear them and maintain friendly relations with them. He wanted now to make a treaty that would be lasting.

We each agreed that in case anything should arise between us, that is my people and his, that was not right, no difference of what nature, whether serious or not, that we were not to take the matter in our own hands and avenge our own cause, but were to refer it to the respectful chiefs and arbitrate our difficulties in case they should arise, instead of avenging our own cause. This was the chief's own proposition. This struck me as a wise course to pursue as we were amongst a race of savages with whom difficulty was liable to arise at any time.

yhen we reached our destination, we went to work and built a fort. Shortly after our arrival, the chief came to me and wanted me to take some men and teams and get some large timbers for a fish trap, telling me there would be fish, plenty for them and us both, and if I would get the large timbers they would make the wicket work and we would all fish together. This suited the President, so he sent some men with me and we got out the large timbers while they were making the wicket work.

When the trap was finished, the chief told me to come early the next morning, for the fish were already there and the Indians were hungry. Accordingly, I went up to the trap as soon as it was light, taking Brother B. F. Cummings with me, as he had requested me to call him when I went.

When we got there, there were about fifty Indians waiting on the bank of the river for me to come. The chief chided me for being late, saying the Indians were very hungry and were not allowed to catch anything until I had caught the first fish; then they could catch, but not before. So the chief and I fixed our hooks and stepped out on the platform, the chief waiting for me to catch the first before he was allowed to catch any. I had a large pole about 12 feet long for my fish pole with a hook about four inches across and a socket to run my pole into with a piece of lariat tied to my hook in such a manner as to allow my hook to pull off of my pole and then the fish would hang by the lariat and could not break my pole.

The bull pen, as I called it, was full of fish, some of them three to four feet in length. When I got ready there were four very large ones swimming close to me, so I made a grab at one and caught him in the side, but he was so large and heavy and I jerked so hard that I tore him for very nigh a foot. My hoot came out so suddenly that the end of my pole caught an Indian that was standing behind me right by the side of his nose and knocked him down as dead, to all appearance, as if a cannon ball had struck him. In the excitement, I did not know I had hit anything, but as I was fixing my hook to try again the chief said to me, "Look at that Indian you have killed."

I looked and saw him lying there sure enough. I asked the chief what killed him; he said I hit him in the eye. I went and examined him and saw I had hit him by the side of the nose. I felt of his pulse but he had none, so I went to work chafing him, but seemingly to no purpose for some time. Finally he came to and I went back to my fishing, but Brother Cummings was very uneasy and kept insisting that we must go, but I would not go until I had caught five. Brother Cummings declared he would not help to carry more than two and when I quit fishing and got a pole to hang them on he would not allow but two to be put on the pole, he was in such a hurry to get away for fear of the Indians.

So I gave three that I had caught to the chief and left my hook with him for him to fish with as it was better than his, and told the chief when the Indian got smart (well) enough to tell him to come up and I would make him some presents, as I did not want to hurt him and did not want him to feel bad. He said he should not feel bad, that he had no business behind me, that I had no eyes in the back of my head.

In three or four days after this, the Indian came to see me and I gave him some presents, and the Indians being about to start to the buffalo country, I advised him to stay with us, telling him that I would take care of him until he would get well, that I was afraid that if he went to the buffalo country that so much traveling on horseback would kill him, as the bones were all broken clear through his head. But he thought he could stand it, but he could not, and died in a few days out. This was almost one of my first adventures, but the Indians never had any ill feelings towards me about it, not in the least degree, knowing it was purely accidental.

~AP~

CHAPTER 13

GEORGE WASHINGTON HILL
(5X) Great Grandpa

LANGUAGE

We had a great many Nez Perces visit us that summer, and they all took quite a liking to me. There was one in particular named Clark, a half-breed son of Clark of Clark and Lewis Journal, with bright red hair, blue eyes, and as thin skin as you would see on any man. He always called me his Little Brother because I was the same complexion he was and he was a little older. He would always come and stay with me when they would be there and take all the pains imaginable with me to teach me the Nez Perce language. I made wonderful progress in the language while they would be with us.

Quite late in the fall, the Indians began to come in for winter quarters. There was one came in that had a very sick little girl. The Indians that I had baptized on the way out told him that we administered to the sick, anointing them and praying over them, so he came after me to go and administer to her. I told him we did not make a practice of administering to people that did not belong to the Church, and if we went and administered to her and she got well, we would expect him to be baptized. He said that was a bargain.

So I took Brothers Cummings and Moore and went out to their camp and administered to the child who was burning up, as it were, with fever, and before we took our hands off of her head, the sweat broke out in great drops all over her face and she was well at once.

The following Sunday there was quite a crowd of Indians at our meeting and after we got through, the President called on me to preach to the Indians, which I tried to do in my weak way, telling them that if they believed, that we would baptize them if they wanted it, when they all cried out, "I do!" "I do!" all over the crowd. So we went to the water and I baptized fifty-six.

When I had baptized the men, as is the custom with Indians for the men to all take the lead, the water being very cold, the President said to me I had better come out and let someone else baptize the women. I came out and told them that one of the brethren would baptize the rest. They refused to come, saying if I did not baptize them they would not be baptized. At this I told them to come along and I would baptize them, which I did.

This raised a jealousy and envy against me amongst the brethren which continued to grow as long as the mission continued, for although they would not try to learn to talk or do anything with the Lamanites, still when they came to me and demanded baptism at my hands and I would go to the water and attend to it, they would say, "Oh, there is nobody here that can baptize the Indians but George," when in truth, the Indians would not go to any of them for baptism nor be baptized by them. In fact, when the old chief Tiar-en-do, or Mog as he was called by white men, came for baptism, the President said that he would baptize the Indians that day. It was all that I could do to get them to let him baptize them. Says they, "We want you to baptize us." I told them they were chiefs and it was good for them to be baptized by our chief.

It was very hard work for them to give up, but by hard persuasion they finally consented and were baptized by him. On this mission I baptized some one hundred eight or ten, but this envy and jealousy continued to grow and increase, and while I was improving every opportunity for getting their language and paying the Indians to stop with me and teach me, and at the same time offering all the boys to come to me and I would teach them all I had learned free gratis, and that I would be glad to do so, they would not take advantage of the offer and the spirit of jealousy continued throughout the mission.

[This is the end of the history written by George Washington Hill. The following seems to be notes made after the fact.]

Just before his death 16 January 1850, Richard Hill called his family around him and said, "I am going to leave you, I will never get out of this bed, but before I die I wish to say to you that the message George has brought is true. I want you all to go with him to the mountains and join your lot with that people."

In March 1850, the company consisting of the mother, Sarah Strait Hill; Return Richard Hill and wife, Rhoda, with their children Catherine, Sarah, Newton and Frank; John Strait Hill and William James Hill led by George Washington Hill, came to the valley.

* * * * *

The Endowment House was dedicated 29 October, 1852. George W. Hill and Cynthia were among the first couples to go there. While they were away Grandmother Hill died, 28 Oct. 1852.

They built a house close to theirs on the farm for Sarah Strait Hill, probably 1850 or 51. George Richard used to go in to see her often.

* * * * *

In the spring of 1853, plans were laid for G. W. Hill's adobe home, consisting of three rooms below and two rooms above. So much work hauling wall that it was 1854 before the house was completed. Richard, a mason, doing that part of the work, took sick and died 14 November, 1853.

* * * * *

The following is taken from notes and incidents as remembered by Clarinda Cynthia Hill and given to her daughter, now Mrs. Iva M. Bishop. This incident is also recorded in the book "The Life of Lorenzo Snow," pages 83-84. He was one of the missionary group called by President Brigham Young to open up and carry the gospel message to different fields in Europe. Lorenzo Snow was sent to open up the mission in Italy. It is very interesting to read and compare the two accounts of the same incident.

Upon arrival in the Salt Lake Valley, September 18, 1847, they camped in the Old Fort now known as Pioneer Park. Here they had a little hut with dirt roof and floor. It was in this place on the 19th of October 1848, that their second child, Clarinda Cynthia Hill was born. During this time it was often necessary to put pans on the bed and on the floor to catch the water that leaked through the dirt during rain storms.

Just before they arrived in the Valley (1849, see short note) [this would be George's second time to arrive in the Valley, as he brings his wife's family], Grandfather became anxious to see his family and join them for the July 24th celebration. He took a horse with saddle and went in advance of the others. He testified that while he was riding [walking—he had lost his horse], he knew someone was with him. Several times he turned to speak to the party, but seeing no one, he did not speak. He felt strongly impressed that he had a partner who was there as a protection to him.

George W. Hill spent some twenty-five years as an Indian missionary and friend, spending much of his time in that work. In 1855, he and others were called on a mission to the Indians. Near Fort Hall they met some Indians and conversed with them. Further on their way they were met by a Bannock Chief who said the Great Spirit had told them to meet and welcome the missionaries to his country. They located on the Salmon River and built Fort Lemhi. Grandfather built himself a house in the fort and invited the Indians in. They took a liking to him and taught him their language. He would visit them and eat the food they prepared. He studied their habits and traits of character and gained their love and confidence. Not only did he master the Shoshone language, but he gained a good knowledge of four other tribal languages.

The Indians told Grandfather about an Indian Prophet. He [an Indian speaking to George W. Hill] said, "One time this prophet and a number of Indians were riding by the Salmon River, which was high and swift. As they wondered how they would get over the river, they saw to their surprise the prophet riding up the river on the other side. How he got there they could not tell.

"On another occasion he [the prophet] sat in council with the Indians, telling them of things to come. Suddenly he exclaimed, 'They have killed two of my boys; I must see to that.' He left the tent. They followed, but when they reached the tent door, he was nowhere to be seen, nor could they find his tracks. He suddenly appeared at the scene where the two young Indians had been shot. He took them by the hand and they sprang to their feet and went with him.

"Now," said the Indian, "The prophet says he wants to see you. But if you cannot come, he said to tell you this: 'There will be an army come this year against the Mormons. They will make a fort south of Salt Lake City, but there will be no fighting. After a time there will be other soldiers come from the West. They will make a fort east of Salt Lake City, but there will be no fighting. After a while they will make a fort North of Salt Lake City, but still there will be no fighting. By and by the mountains will be full of soldiers, and then such fighting as the world never saw. He will ask you who I am. Tell him I was chained in the middle of a house. A big storm blew the house down and my chains fell off. I was put in a deep hole to starve to death, but the pit could not hold me. I was bound and thrown into a fire hotter than he ever saw, but the flames never scorched me. I have been placed in dens of wild beasts, but they did not touch me. When you tell him these things, he will know who I am.'"

* * * * *

The following is an article written by Grandfather Hill and published in the Juvenile Instructor as a reprint–August 1954:

COME AND PREACH TO US by George W. Hill

The Indians from down Humboldt, from Battle Mountain, Carlin, Winnemucca and all that section of country (Nevada) for two years had been begging me to come to their country and preach to them. They were visiting me almost continually. With all the chiefs that came, it was the same story: "Come and preach to us, and teach us how to farm and how to live as white people do."

Well, things were in this condition when in the latter part of April, 1873, I was called to this ministry. About the first of May, the chiefs of a band that were encamped on Bear River about twelve miles from Corinne (Utah) paid me a visit. During our talk, they invited me to come out to their camp and preach to them. I promised to do so, but told them I did not know what day I could come as I was the employee of the railroad company at the time [he was night watchman] and did not know when I could get away, but would come as soon as I could. With this promise they went home.

Getting leave of absence for one night on the 5th day of May, 1873, at eight o'clock in the morning, I got aboard the C.P. freight train and went as far as Corinne, where I left the train and started on foot across the prairie, a distance of some 12 miles, to the camp. I had proceeded not more than one mile when I met an old Indian named Tig-we-ticker, who came up laughing and said Ti-guitch, their chief, had told them as soon as he got up that morning that Ink-a-pompy, as they called me, was coming to see them that day, and that they must clean up and all stay at home. He also told them that I was coming on foot and wondered why I did not come with my mules and wagon, as he thought I was getting too old to walk so far.

The old Indian said he was going to Corinne to buy a beef head as he had nothing to eat; he gave me directions to camp and said he would hurry back. So I went on. About three miles further I met Po-pe-ha and another young Indian going to Corinne on the same business as the old man. They came up laughing and told me the same story that the old man had told me. Also they said they would hurry back to the meeting.

I went on, pondering these things over in my mind and asked myself how it was that the old chief could tell so correctly the time I would arrive. It seemed it was done to convince me that the time had come for the work to commence among them, but still it was a mystery to me how he could see me and tell the time of day I would arrive and how I looked and traveled and that, too, correctly.

I was thinking of this when lo and behold, I met the chief coming to bring me a horse to ride to camp. This satisfied me that my Father in Heaven had something to do with it; so I resigned myself into His hands and said, "Father, Thy will be done," believing that these things were done to satisfy me that the time had come for the work to commence among the Indians.

When we arrived in camp, the Indians came together in a few minutes, and I preached to them, even astonishing myself. After meeting we repaired to the water and I baptized and confirmed 102 Indians. After confirmation, I talked to them a while in regard to their duties as the spirit seemed to direct, when I bade them adieu and returned to Corinne in time for the C.P. train. I arrived at Ogden at half past one o'clock the same night, having ridden on the freight train over 50 miles, walked 24 miles, preached to, baptized and confirmed upwards of 100 persons.

* * * * *

In addition to his work among the Indians, Grandfather was a busy man. In moving to Ogden, he purchased a farm where the First Ward was later organized. A fort was built in Ogden, called Brown's Fort, which was a mile square with a wall around it. The people were advised to move into this fort and guards were stationed around it. Grandfather took his turn at this guard duty. He moved into this fort along with the rest.

In 1853, sickness came into the home and Heber James died. Then again on 8 October, 1860, Isaiah Lorenzo died, and they lost a daughter, Ida Rebecca on 5 October 1867.

In 1855 when Grandfather was called to go on the Indian Mission, he rented his farm to his brother who was to furnish the family with firewood and wheat. That summer they had a grasshopper war. The grasshoppers were taking everything in sight. It looked as if everything green was being taken. But a strong east wind came up and as the grasshoppers arose they were blown away. The next day they were all gone, but on the shore of the lake there was a ridge about three feet high. Thus a portion of the crops was saved.

The next winter was a hard one and the people suffered much. New emigrants entered the valley, provisions were short and as this was an extremely cold winter with a lot of snow, they lost many of their cattle. In the spring they went to the mountains in search of segos, thistles, and nettles to cook for food. From May until August there was not sufficient bread in any of the homes. Such were the conditions, and that year President Brigham Young preached reformation among the people. Everyone was called upon to repent and this brought a different state of feeling among the people.

George W. Hill was faithful in the performance of his church duties and was advanced in the priesthood to the office of Patriarch. He was also diligent in providing for his family, many times under difficult circumstances. Later on, he moved to Salt Lake City and worked in the tithing office, as Indian interpreter, and was also a guard around the Church Office.

He was a man of sterling character. He had strong faith and his extraordinary courage in times of hardship and trial are evidences of the real greatness of our grandfather.

The Lord said: "If you keep my commandments and endure to the end, you shall have eternal life, which gift is the greatest of all the gifts of God." Our grandfather was rich in the values that count and was true to the end. He left us a heritage and example worthy of emulation.

He died 24 February 1891. Cynthia Utley Stewart Hill died 8 April 1908.

~MP~
CHAPTER 14

SURPRISE: THE PRIZE IN THE SIR PRIZE
Life Is Such A Precious Gift

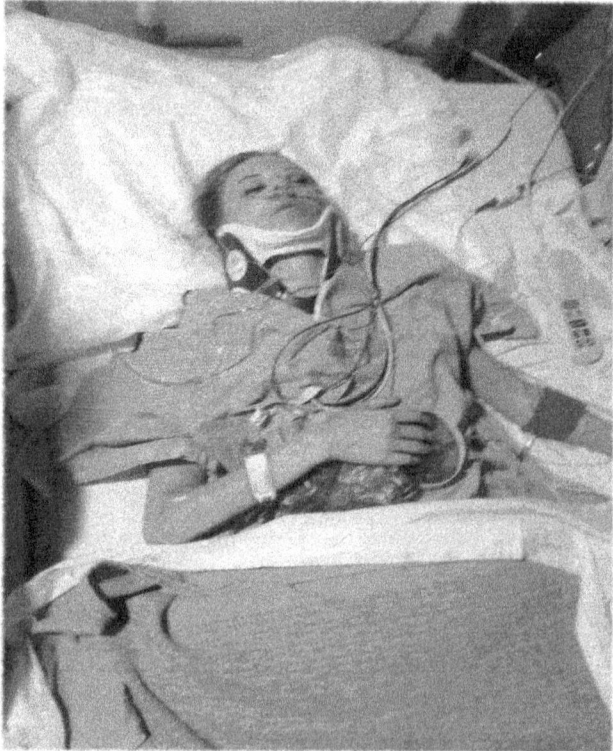

~*Contribution*~

Andi J.

At 29 most of my friends were already married and had started their families. While they were shopping for back to school I was flying to L.A. to work with celebrities. When they were taking trips to the park I was taking trips to Thailand. They drove a minivan and I rode on an elephant.... everything about my life was the polar opposite of theirs and I couldn't imagine ever wanting it to be any different...

It's funny how quickly things can change. I rolled out of bed, at my usual 10 am start time and started to get ready for the day. Since I do promotional modeling I get paid as much in one weekend as I would normally make working a full-time job. I tend to only work about 8 days a month and I loved the freedom it afforded me. I was working a business to business event at the conference center so I had to wear a dress and heels. I quickly got dressed and left for the event. It was a long day but I had fun.

I walked out to my car to drive home but my feet were killing me from wearing heels all day and they were really tall so I was hesitant to drive in them. Luckily I had a pair of sneakers in my car. I put them on.

They looked ridiculous with my nice dress but I didn't care because I was just going to drive home and nobody was going to see me. I was driving along and I remembered that I needed to stop by the client's office to pick up my pay for the day, but I never made it.

I had to get off the freeway on an exit that was under a lot of construction. The ramp was torn up and they had it barreled off so that the exit was extremely short and narrow.

As I started to go for the ramp I hit some gravel and since I was slowing in preparation for the exit it made my car slide a bit toward one of the construction barrels. I didn't know what they were made of (plastic: ok to hit or cement: Will crush you to death) so I swerved to avoid it. For, the record, the barrels are not made of cement so go ahead and hit them if the situation arises. It'll do far less damage than the alternative! Well, swerving on a narrow ramp is obviously a terrible idea, and it had me aimed right at the cement barrier separating the ramp from the freeway. At that point, there was no avoiding it. I knew I was going to crash into something. In my last ditch effort to minimize the impact I tried to hit the brakes and spin my car a bit to avoid hitting the wall head-on.

It all happened really fast but it felt like it was going in slow motion. I spun the car as much as I could as I watched the wall get closer and closer. At the last second before impact I ducked to the side, leaning my body between the gear shift and center console. Then I hit the wall. There was a flash of red and then everything went black.

When I opened my eyes the dust from the airbag was still settling. Thankfully no one else was in my car, I was not on my phone, and no other people were involved. Just me vs a cement barrier and the barrier won! The end of the barrier crunched up the driver side door leaving just a triangle of space that somehow I was lucky enough to get wedged into. Part of the door crunched in and my leg/hip was pinned under it and the seat crunched and squished me too. I was pushed to the side by the crooked seat and the bar that used to make up the door frame.

The airbags were hanging out and had a bit of blood on them. I felt like I was pretty logical in the situation but looking back now I think I underestimated just how hard I hit my head! Instead of freaking out my first thought (after checking to make sure there were no other people involved obviously) was to do an inventory of my car. I just bought new tires, new spark plugs and wires, AND a brand new windshield. I was pretty mad that all the money was going to go to waste but I was very happy to see that my windshield was still in pristine condition. I still had the receipt and fully intended to return it. In my mind that made perfect sense at the time.

I could feel blood running down my face and my head was a little sore so I did a quick mental check on my body. I was having a hard time getting a full breath but I wasn't alarmed because I thought I just knocked the wind out of myself and it would correct itself after a bit. I wiggled my toes first and they moved. I could feel all my body parts and was able to move my hands, arms, head/neck, etc. without problem all except for my knee. It was pinned between the crushed in door and the seat. I thought that I could just wiggle my way out but as I tried to pull my leg out it wouldn't budge. I pulled as hard as I could and I pushed against the door but nothing was working. That's when I started to panic a little bit. I was trapped!

My eyes were watering a bit but my salty tears hurt the cuts on my face so I was trying to stay calm and not cry. All of a sudden in the middle of that panic I felt the most peaceful feeling rush through my body.

I had only ever experienced that one other time in my life and I instantly knew everything was going to be ok. I didn't know how, because I had no savings to my name, I just totaled my only form of transportation, and I was not going to be able to work for a while. By all standards, I had every reason to be panicked.

My life was in complete chaos and yet I felt calm. I quit pushing on the door and as I glanced up I noticed there was a man sitting in my passenger seat. He kind of looked like Hector Elizondo and he was wearing khakis with a long sleeve white shirt and a forest green microfleece vest over top of it. He asked me if I was ok and I told him that I thought I was. Then he asked if I knew who hit me. Instantly I was confused. I started to wonder how long I had really been unconscious because I THOUGHT I had been awake for just about all of it but I didn't remember hitting anybody. A hundred scenarios ran through my head, did someone hit me from behind, did I slide and hit someone else, did I somehow fly over the barrier and cause a massive car pile up for people trying to avoid me?! I was terrified that other people were hurt. I started to panic again.

Did you hit me? I asked him. No, he replied. I let out a sigh of relief. Then I told him, I'm stuck in here and I can't get out. I pushed on the door again and it didn't budge. I could feel my heart starting to race and it was getting harder and harder to breathe. In a very calm voice, he reassured me that I was okay.

The ambulance is on their way he said. I calmed down again. I knew he was right. Help was on the way and they would push the car away from the wall so I could get out and I would be ok. I leaned back on my seat and closed my eyes to try and keep my heart rate down and breathing even.

I never heard the man leave but when I opened my eyes there were firefighters standing on the hood of my car yelling back and forth to each other. They used the jaws of life to cut the entire top off of my car. To my devastation that destroyed the windshield, I was going to replace haha.

After the roof was cut off and peeled back like a giant sardine can a bunch of firemen and EMT's gathered around me. They told me they were going to push a stretcher down in behind my back, strap me to it, and pull me out, which they did. I was really frustrated that I was strapped in because I felt like my breathing would be better if I could just roll onto my side.

Inside the ambulance, they started to cut my dress off but I begged the girl not to because I really liked it. She kindly cut it down the side seam so I could re-sew it. It was a very nice gesture, considering it was covered in blood that would never come out and the back was shredded to pieces. You've really got to appreciate the little details. People can be pretty cool especially when they humor your delusional requests without acting like you're insane. The 2 emt's in the ambulance immediately got to business checking me and they put on a really obnoxious neck brace.

I heard one of them mention pneumothorax which I recognized as a collapsed lung thanks to all the medical dramas I had been watching with grandma. (see, sometimes you learn relevant things from television) I was in good spirits all the way to the hospital and I was cracking jokes the whole time despite the lack of oxygen. I really didn't think things were that bad. When they wheeled me in through the er doors some people gasped and had horrified looks on their faces. That's when I realized I must have looked horrible. I tried my best to look alive and well to show everyone I was ok.

They got me into a room to prep for surgery where one other guy (who was not looking so hot) was also waiting, both of us were still on our stretchers. They finally unstrapped me and I immediately rolled onto my side. A nurse rushed over to me and kept trying to get me to stay on my back but I didn't care. It felt so good to finally breathe! She came back with a few other people and they put one of those annoying tubes in my nose. A doctor or nurse (I'm not sure) came over and looked at my face. He told me he could see the bone so they started stitching....except they forgot to numb it!!! I was kind of wincing with every stitch and part way through he said, "wait, can you feel this?" and I was like "Uh, YEAH!" So they got me numbed up and finished stitching.

At that point, a nurse was trying to get a phone number from me to contact family and I could not for the life of me remember anyone's number except for my childhood friend Matt.

Then a doctor came in and told me I needed to go to surgery to place a tube for my collapsed lung (no surprise there) and that I also needed surgery because I broke my pelvis. Confused I told him that he must be mistaking me for the battered guy in the waiting room because I didn't have a broken pelvis. Thank goodness the car had pinned me in during the accident because I genuinely thought I was fine and I would have tried to walk had I been able to.

While I was waiting to go into surgery my family started to show up. I felt bad because they looked so sad because of me and I felt fine. I wished they had cleaned me up a little before they called my family because I was still covered in blood and glass and banged up and I knew that scared them. I scared one nurse to death when she was taking my blood and accidentally poked herself. She told me it's policy to do an HIV and hep c test after that. I told her that was a good idea because I pierced my bellybutton in an alley, under the stairs, in Thailand. She had me signing consent forms before I even finished my sentence They also decided that would be a good time to do a pregnancy test just for good measure.

Then a police officer came to take my statement. I thought I was fairly coherent, but looking back at my scribble of a signature right across the middle of his statement page I would have to say I was still pretty out of it.
I later looked up the police records for my accident with all the other witness statements. Everything written was as I remembered it EXCEPT, there was no statement from a man and nobody mentions him being there or being in my car.

That leads me to believe he may have been my guardian angel...but I also kinda hope he's not because if he is then I accused him of hitting me when all he was doing was trying to look out for me. If he's my guardian angel the poor guy has already been working overtime as it is! All in all, I cut my face and arm, Lacerated my spleen, broke some ribs, collapsed my lung, broke my scapula and broke my pelvis. It took some stitches, a breathing tube, and pelvic surgery to piece me back together. Our running joke was that even though I broke a bunch of bones it was ok because the blood test had come back negative so I wasn't pregnant.

When I got wheeled to my room after surgery I was still making jokes and trying to show off my single sister's photo to all of the cutest medical staff. I knew my family was scared because they were acting really careful around me like they thought I would break and I could see how scared they were. I was pretty tired so everyone started to leave and mom decided to stay the night with me which was nice of her. During the night I woke up and I was just laying in the dark looking around the room. It was just lit up by the lights from on the monitors and I could hear all the machines beeping and pumping etc. All of a sudden I thought I heard a huge juicy fart! I started to laugh really hard because I thought mom was letting them rip in her sleep. I had to try really hard to control it because every time I laughed it hurt from all the broken ribs.

The next day I realized it wasn't mom making that noise all night it was fluid in the breathing tube so I cracked myself up over my own machine.

[My sister] showed up right after breakfast and offered to help me shower which was really nice. My back was super itchy and I thought it was because of the lack of showering until they went to lift me up into my wheelchair (which would be my new wheels for the next few months) and my entire back was covered in broken glass. I was still sitting on the sheet that had been used in pulling me out of my car so there was still broken glass underneath of me. My sweet sister helped me dig it all out and then helped me wash the blood and glass out of my hair and get cleaned up. I felt more like a person and less like a scary monster after that. Tons of friends and family members came to visit me in the hospital and I feel like that helped me to heal faster.

I was supposed to be in the hospital for a few weeks and then rehab for months but I only ended up being in the hospital for 5 days and then got transferred right away to a brand new rehabilitation facility that was taking on 18 patients for free to get the word out about their facility. As a person with no insurance and a daily shot that cost $100 per shot I greatly appreciated it! I wasn't supposed to use the wheelchair much before I left the hospital but the morning after surgery

 I asked if I could wheel myself around the hall. The dr was hesitant but he told me we could give it a try. I wore myself out but I made it all the way to the end of the hall and back. By the time I went to the rehabilitation center I was wheeling myself most places and showering myself and moving back and forth from my bed to my wheelchair.

Everything seemed to be going great. While I had no job, no car, no savings, and a massive hospital bill, with substantial injuries I still felt optimistic. I didn't know how it would work out but I knew everything was going to be ok. at the rehab facility, we had a fun family game night and I got to visit with more of my friends.

I butted heads with the staff a time or two being my usual stubborn self. Sometimes I refused to go to morning sessions because I was literally SO exhausted! I couldn't figure out why I was so tired but I thought it must just be left over from the accident. I found myself getting overly emotional about things as well. I was easily irritated over small things.

One example is the 4 pm dinner time. I HATED eating that early and was never very hungry at that time. One night I had a particularly rough therapy session and my friends had been kicked out for the night due to visiting hours and the dr was lecturing me because I hadn't gone down to the cafeteria for dinner. "It's a long time until morning and you won't have anything to eat. The kitchen closes at blah blah blah." I tuned him out because I wasn't in the mood for a lecture.

After he left the room I stubbornly grabbed my laptop, googled the nearest Jimmy John's and placed a delivery order. They had my dinner there in under 10 minutes and my doctor just gave an exasperated sigh when he brought it to my room.

It wasn't just irritability either. Sometimes at dinner, I would just start crying for no real reason, but in a place like that nobody questions you if your crying. We are all going through some pretty tough physical stuff to be there in the first place. I cried over Tom and Jerry because they really could have been great friends if they just stopped fighting and one night alone in my room I watched Dumbo and just bawled my eyes out. The way he looked at his mom, and she looked at him just left me with the most hollow, and lonely feeling I had ever experienced in my life.

I cried at night sometimes when I was alone and I cried at every bell ceremony (When people were ready to leave the facility we all went out into the hall and made a long line and clapped for them as they came down the hallway. At the end, right by the door there was a bell and they would ring it before they left to go home) I wasn't sure if I was crying because I was happy for them, or sick of being there, or homesick, or maybe just a mixture of all of it. I cried when a man who had been a bishop took his first steps.

He had been in the facility for a long time and it was putting a big strain on his family. They didn't know if he was going to be able to walk again and the diagnosis had been pretty grim. Then one day while we were all in the therapy room He stood up, holding onto the handrails on both sides of him and without help from anyone he took three steps! He had to sit down after but he did it himself and I remember being so happy for him I just started crying at the table while I finished my exercises. Nobody else at that table had dry eyes either though.

When I talked to my doctor about being so emotional he told me that can happen after a trauma. The lack of a period could be blamed on all the weight I'd lost post accident and stress. The sleeping, stress and rebuilding strength. Every symptom could be explained away by the accident and that's what all the doctors did. I finally left the rehab facility and rang the bell for myself. I was nervous to go home and back to the real world in a wheelchair but I was glad I had a lot of people to help and support me and I coincidentally lived with my grandparents in a house that was wheelchair accessible because of the little boy who had lived there before us. Grandma borrowed a wheelchair from Uncle Chuck.

My neighbor who is also in a wheelchair was really nice to hang out with me and give me tips on how to get around and do things (like laundry). We also got a bunch of supplies, like the shower bench, for free from a non-profit organization in Brigham. Everything was just really falling into place. Then one day something weird happened.
I lost a lot of weight after the accident and I had already been skinny to begin with, so I was trying really hard to gain it back.

Usually this is a big struggle for me but after a while, it seemed to be working. I was gaining weight little by little. So on this sunny morning, I woke up and got some yogurt and a banana like I had done every morning for the past month or so. After eating I headed to the bathroom to attempt a shower but while I was in there I got really sick very suddenly and threw up.

When I came out of the bathroom I told grandma that she shouldn't eat the bananas or yogurt because they gave me food poisoning. It seemed a bit weird since I didn't think yogurt could really go bad, and the banana wasn't mushy, but I brushed it off. Later that day we were having a family barbecue and everyone was over at the house. Grandma had a frozen pineapple and she decided to microwave it to speed up the thawing process. I was clear on the other side of the room but the smell of it instantly made me sick. That's when I knew there had to be a mistake. Lots of things seemed off and people were able to explain it away by blaming it on the accident but you don't develop supersonic smelling powers from a car accident.

I suspected the hospital was wrong about the pregnancy test so I quietly took my sister aside and told her what I thought was going on. She agreed to drive me to the hospital but it was a weekend so I had to go to the urgent care.
She felt really bad leaving me there in my wheelchair to wheel myself in alone but I had no idea what they were going to say or how long it was going to take so I sent her home and went in by myself. I sat and waited for a few hours since it wasn't a huge emergency. I teared up when a boy came in with his mom and dad. He looked terrified but didn't cry.

He was trying to be so brave. I could see they had a towel wrapped around his hand. The dad had a tense jaw and the mom looked like she was fighting back tears. At one point a nurse came out to look at his hand and they had to unwrap it.

I could see his hand was covered in blood and his fingers were in terrible shape. The boy couldn't keep it in anymore. His lip started to tremble and big tears rolled down his cheeks. My heart broke for him. I sat in my wheelchair praying that he would be ok and would feel better soon. His dad gave him the biggest hug and just held him until he stopped crying. I wish I knew what happened to that boy.

They finally came and got me and did a test which came back positive then had me wait in another room until a nurse could come for an ultrasound. It was like, "hey great news you get to be out of the wheelchair soon, but your also pregnant." It felt like it took forever for someone to come tell me what was going on! When the nurse finally came in she asked how far along

I thought I was and I couldn't even tell her. I thought maybe it was a freak symptom of the accident or at most I would see a little blob but when she put the machine on my belly

I saw a FACE!!

He was actually moving around and was easily recognizable as a baby. I heard the heartbeat but it sounded really slow. I thought babies had really fast heartbeats so I asked her if the heartbeat was mine or the baby's and she said it was the baby's. I asked her if it was too slow and if he was ok but she said she couldn't make comments about the ultrasound only a doctor could.

Then she wheeled me back into my room where I spent an excruciating time thinking about all the things that could be wrong to cause a slow heartbeat. Was the baby there during the accident? Was it injured? Could the stress harm or kill it? What about the medication and multiple surgeries and radiation from all the xrays? I tried to prepare myself for bad news. That my baby was hurt or something was developmentally wrong, or worse, not going to make it. When the doctor came in he said he thought things were ok but I needed to check with an obstetrician and with the hospital radiation specialist to figure out what the radiation dosage may have been.

Eventually, the radiologist called me back and told me it should be ok. I got the proper prenatal care that I needed and even though there were a few crazy incidents while I had to sneak around I eventually told all my family and was able to relax a little bit. I worried that I would miscarry or that my baby would be born with 3 eyeballs or severe developmental issues but on a beautiful December day I had a beautiful little boy and he was perfect. He is a sweet, calm baby, and he seems like he was just born knowing how to handle everything. In great chaos, a miracle was born and it righted everything. Since I was pregnant during the car accident the hospital stay for that and for my son's birth were all covered.

The rehab just happened to be accepting new patients for free and I was one of them. The house was wheelchair accessible. I got the supplies I needed....everything about him just has a way of working itself out. He filled that emptiness I had in ways I never knew I wanted or needed. He came here in a whirlwind but it was EXACTLY the way it was all supposed to be.

~AP~
CHAPTER 15

THE DECEIVER- Truly a wicked step mother

Great Great Great Grandmother-
Life Sketch of Mary Jane Simpson Gould Fuller
18 December 1861 – 20 January 1911

Compiled by daughters: Annabelle Wilson and Dora Fuller and retold by great great great Grandson-G.B.- Family Tree

Mary Jane was born the third child of Robert and Joan Simpson Gould in Salt Lake City, Utah. Her parents had only been in Salt Lake three months. They came from Scotland and had crossed the plains in the company of Mormons. They did not stay in Salt Lake City long, but as many saints did, they obeyed the command of church leaders to help settle towns throughout Utah. The family moved to Ogden, then to Liberty, and then to Eden, all in Weber County.

The home of the Gould's in Ogden Valley was not unlike their neighbors; it had a dirt floor, was made of logs and had a fireplace for cooking and heat. Mary was a small delicate child who needed protection and loving care from her mother. This was not to be for the black haired, brown eyed Mary. When she was eight years old her mother died and thus began the turmoil. Her father soon married again, perhaps thinking that he had someone who could make a good home for his family. Elizabeth Eule Gould became her step-mother. She was a cruel woman without the knowledge of caring for a family nor the patience to teach children. When the children did not respond immediately to her demands she would beat them and give them even more difficult work to do. Much of the work they were given was beyond their childhood strength to perform.

On one occasion when Mary's father came home unexpectedly, he found the step-mother holding Mary by her hair and was about to cut the child's throat with a kitchen knife. This brought her father to the realization that the reported stories of the children were true. In an effort to escape the extreme discipline practiced by the step-mother,

Mary and her sister, Elizabeth, went away from the home to work as soon as they were able. Mary was fortunate to find work in the home of Elizabeth Boyle in Ogden. Mrs. Boyle was a kind and considerate person in assigning duties to young Mary. She was pleased with her work and had deep compassion for her. She interceded in Mary's behalf when the step-mother requested that she return home as she was needed there to help with the work. Later, Mary went back to Eden to work for Mrs. Constance Eggleston. She enjoyed working for Mrs. Eggleston as there was a mutual affection between them and Mary was learning much from these experiences.

When Mary was eighteen years old she left the Eggleston home to be married to Henry John Fuller. She was given a joyous welcome into the Fuller family. Henry's mother was especially happy to have Mary in the family as she had known her through the years she had lived and worked in Eden. The marriage was truly one of love and devotion. Although they started out living in a small two room house, built by Henry, with meager furnishings, they acquired enough to raise a large family of eleven children.

In their home was a happy and loving atmosphere where children learned love and affection for each other. They learned the value of work, the need for education and the joy of sharing in social, civic and religious activities. Mary delighted the children in their early years by playing games with them, taking them on picnics and during the long winter evenings they would read and enjoy music together. In October of 1900 there was a very sad event in the family, William the oldest son, died. On the same day, October 23rd Mary gave birth to a new daughter, Arvilla.

The long days of nursing William prior to his death, coupled with her own physical discomfort with the pregnancy was a very nervous and exhausting period for Mary. She was bed fast with nervous prostration for sometime following the death of William and the birth of Arvilla. The older sisters at home took responsibility for the home and care of the baby during this time. In due time, she did recover to some extent and had two more children.

Mary was always religious and believed in the answer to prayers. This was a help to her many times in her life. She was baptized a member of the L.D.S. Church 15 June 1869 by John Farrell. She was confirmed by Richard Ballentyne. She served as a visiting teacher in the Relief Society. In 1892 she became the second counselor to Sarah Ann Carver in the YWMIA. On 27 June 1895 she became a counselor to Sarah I. Shupe in the Relief society, a position she held until 13 December 1908. Her husband, Henry was called to be the Bishop of the Eden Ward, 15 June 1895.

Mary went to Alberta, Canada during the late summer of 1910. She went to visit her sister, Elizabeth McBride. Although her daughter, Roseltha Burnett, went along to take care of her, she was exhausted when she returned to Eden. She had a re-occurrence of the nervous prostration and was in bed until the first week of January, 1911.

It was then that her husband was confined with typhoid-pneumonia. With great will-power and special effort, she cared for him until his death on 13 January 1911. At this time she collapsed and was bed fast until her death one week later, 20 January 1911.

~MP~
CHAPTER 16

Grandparents are Brilliant!

THEY'VE FOUND A NEW WAY TO HAVE KIDS

CHAPTER 16
ANCIENT PIONEER CONTRIBUTION
GRANDPARENTS ARE BRILLIANT
They've Found a New Way to Have Kids
Gary Reed Burnett

Love in the home-Hope, courage, and determination to keep going and enjoy the journey.

I hope that this perspective will give insight to those of you who may be going through similar circumstances and courage to face whatever challenges lay ahead.

I am the second oldest of my ten siblings and the oldest boy. I have had the opportunity of sharing in the raising of six wonderful children and also have discovered it takes a TRIBE to do so, and now enjoy the great and fun experiences of grandchildren.

"Grandparents are Brilliant!
They've found a new way to have Kids"
   ~GB~

Now consequently, I have an even greater appreciation for my parents for their willingness to sacrifice for our family and their overwhelming perseverance in the face of so much opposition that comes with the territory of having a family, and a very large one at that. I think if you ask my parents they will tell you that the larger number was actually a little easier because they made the comment that the secret sauce was to get the 1st one going in the right direction and then they can show their siblings what to do, and pass it on.

. I am eternally grateful for parents that did not give up even when at times it must have seemed like their burdens were too much to bare, or the relentless trials and tribulation must have looked insurmountable at times.

Because my parents were willing to persevere and keep going even in the midst of adversity, such as child birth, cloth diapers, diaper pails, poop, poop, and more poop, and then when we are older, we move out and double our problems by adding more individuals to the mix with adult problems instead of kid problems, just to list a few. They have not only changed our diapers, but the very core of who we are. and the lives of our children and their posterity through enduring and loving examples forever. Perfect?...No, but getting closer everyday.

Upon reflection of my childhood I look back with fondness and admiration for the level of commitment and dedication my parents had for each other and for each of their children. I always felt loved and I knew that my parents wanted to provide me with opportunities that would further my abilities and help me grow. I had what I would consider an idyllic childhood. Maybe too good to be true.

At a young age, my parents encouraged us to develop our talents. They provided us with many opportunities such as art, music, and dance and to enhance our skills, and I remember in my very early years learning to work alongside my father and grandfather, and grandmother and mother on construction projects. I have fond memories of our house on Cahoon at the base of the majestic foothills of the Utah Mountains. A reservoir was our neighbor to the east, and on a couple of occasions we got to watch in fascination as our parents tried to fight the floodwaters and soon just had to open the basement door and watch the knee deep fast flowing river run through it. It was really cool! (for us).

When we were little we enjoyed building snowmen with Dad that were taller than him (6') and upon finishing this amazing and magnificent creation I was lifted by my strong father to rest upon this 'magnificent giant and felt as if I was on top of the world.

Dad is a brilliant man (or at least he had us all believing he is because I am about 60 and even knowing all that I know now he still knows so much more in his little pinky. Discussions about anything and everything with Dad is always a treat Expounding on everything is a fun subject because you don't ever **have to worry about getting off the subject. You can ramble all you want to, and Oh how we love to ramble. You probably noticed.**

Growing up, my parents were conscientious and hardworking and always set high expectations for themselves. They took exceptional effort to make sure that all of us were always up and reading scriptures in the morning and were very tolerant as we came dragging in our pillows and blankets and trying to wipe the sandman out of our eyes with little success. I don't remember much about the scriptures, but I do remember how important my parents thought the daily routine was.

FATHERS

Now that I am a father, I get the importance of consistency. I am awed at the immense effort that was taken to make sure we all had that time together before Dad would have to shuttle out the door to work.. I am certain that for Mom to get ten children out the door all dressed and ready to go for school church or any other activity would have been quite the feat for any parent to achieve.

My parents were always there for us. Just one example of this would be the fishing trip that we took to the Weber River and Dad was in a suit having just put work on hold, but just rolled up his pant legs, grabbed a net, and started scooping out ten pound lunkers at the fish step, because we were not having too much luck as we dangled treble hooks into the falls, but we did get a few and loved fishing.

Or the Family Home Evening, again, he rolls up the suit pant legs, puts on roller skates and he's off and wheeling. Amazingly enough, He would put in a very very long day starting early in the morning scripture study, then off to the military base where he was a top notch Contract Price Analyst, then to work at the (big) family furniture store that my great greats started in the 1800s while Utah was still a territory. My Great Grandfather was a casket maker and as the pioneers stopped dying off he transitioned into fine furniture to the point it was the biggest Union Fleet in the state, and I was running into people that had bought their furniture there in all the four corner states and the west up into Washington as well.

Dad would work late into the night, many times all night and I would go visit him and remember falling asleep

under the 190 characters per minute bi-directional console printer that was running and spitting out his reports all night and all day long.
I will demonstrate the printer for you.

Zzzzhhhh zhhhhhh zzhzhhzh zhhzzzzh zzhz zh zh zhhhzzzt

(it was so advanced it would start back the other way!)

zh zh zhhhzzz zzhz zh zh zhhhzzz zzhz zh zh zhhhzzz ZZZT!

My father was a hard worker and it was so difficult to try and keep up with him because he was my hero of coarse. I must admit I do not remember meeting anyone in my life that impresses me more than my Dad. Never heard him swear, didn't ever drink, smoke, and always a gentleman to my mother.. Did they ever disagree or argue? Sure, but they had a rule and they shared it with us on their 50th wedding anniversary cruise which we got to go on. Wahoo!
That secret was prayer. It is very difficult to be mad at your spouse, and have a conversation with deity. I struggled with this in latter years because I remember coming home and we were both tired so we said casually,

"Who's turn is it tonight?

"T think it's yours"

"I'm quite sure it's yours"

"Well let's just say our own private prayers and go to bed"

"Ok"

That's what I remember about the end of a twenty year marriage. I owe my former spouse (I don't think X is very respectful, so we will use former spouse) an apology for not stepping up to the plate and saying couples prayers no matter who's turn it is. I remember thinking it was no big deal at the time.

Mmmmm so what do you think? A mistake? Yep fraid so!

Some things are not in our control no matter how much we wish they were different. That being said, my parents are perfect examples of someone who has been able to learn from their past.

TOMATOES

I remember the story of the tomato and mom was at the store with dad and was having those strange cravings that come during pregnancies, and that moment she felt a huge sensation that she could not live another minute without a tomato.

She picked it up and was salivating, but realized that she did not put this tiny little red delicious gem into the budget, but was thinking,
"Oh, surely I deserve this and it's just this little tomato."
Well it was the middle of winter and the price of tomatoes was WAY HIGH, but Dad just responded,

"You can have that tomato if you really want it, but you are eating the money we are saving for our house. Do you really want that? You're right, it is just a little tomato."

Mom took the tomato out of her cart, pinched her lip and reluctantly and sadly and longingly placed it back on the shelf.

She still remembers that tomato, but she also remembers sticking to a budget and how wonderful it was to be a home owner. Car owner, and more and more and more because they learned together how to keep a budget together. Did they ever make mistakes?... Yes, but they will tell you that you will come up twice as fast if you make those choices and decisions together as a team.

They taught us about fasting and tithing and how great blessings can come from these.

FASTING

We were very young at the time my grandmother came to the door and announced that our uncle was in a terrible train accident, and the family will be fasting for him.

He was working a rail car on the side track when a moving train unhitched a car while still moving and sent the rail car moving down that track he was on. My uncle was on the roof making repairs and happened to see almost too late the oncoming disaster and tried to jump into the air so that he would be airborne during the crash. Slight miscalculation, and he ended up being smashed between the two and suspended upside down with one leg almost mashed off. Pinned and yelling for help he struggled to stay calm and conscious, but to no avail.

He hung there a very long time passing in and out from loss of blood. They got him to the hospital and the doctor told my Grand Mother and Aunt that he would very likely need to amputate the leg and there were many problems including gangrene was setting in and it was not looking good.

My grandma was very upset and told him not to cut the leg off, but he interrupted her in saying

"You don't seem to understand. The leg is the last worries. I am not sure he is even going to be with us by morning. We will be operating, so you say your prayers for us too. This is not good. Not good at all. You need to pray for his very life that is hanging in the balance and the gangrene has traveled into the trunk of his body, so please reconcile he may not be with us much longer. He is holding onto dear life."

We fasted and sure enough, My uncle lived. He lived into his 80's and was so fun when we would go water skiing at Pinevew reservoir... and man could my uncle slalom!

Years later when he went to work as a security guard and hiss leg was bothering him so he popped it off, and a coworker said" "Hey that's a cool trick. How do you do that?" His coworker never even knew his leg was gone even after knowing him for a long time.
Fasting really works!

TITHING

Because Mom and Dad showed us tithing at a young age it was a snap, and came in real handy when teaching math, and percentages, but was really easy until I got older and had a family and the usual life problems hit the fan. The kind that can test us to the core like Job.

There were massive layoffs, and I was out of work. This was a terrible blow to our young family and we didn't know where to even come up with the money to put food on the table. I was a ward clerk and I realized we were getting behind on tithing and I may not get to be a clerk anymore. I went to the bishop and asked what to do.

He was a kind man, and he gave me the answer that all good bishop's do, and that is I won't tell you what you have to do, but I will share with you that I have seen great blessings come to those that pay their tithing, and shared the scripture that there won't be even enough room to receive it, and then had me visit with my neighbor who was in the bishopric and also a CPA for a profession.

The friend said, "Pay your tithing first and the rest will work out", and proceeded to show me a path to how it could work with a lot of faith.

Because I was a full tithe payer, the bishop was able to help out with the food and to place a food order. That still didn't tale care of the house payment. I was sweating bullets, but when leaving the old job something amazing happened and there was just enough money in a non vested retirement account that was kicked out to me in a lump sum check to take care of the house, the back tithing, and even the food, and I walked into an interview, and got hired immediately, so that we didn't even miss a beat! Not 1 Lick!

The other people from work had the same issues and talked to consumer credit and were advised that you do not have money for charitable contributions, so that's the first thing they cut. It was not so favorable for my coworkers , and I felt bad for them that it did not work out too well.

So at a young age we were expected to work and take care of ourselves. 10 kids and that is a lot of work unless everyone steps up to the plate and takes on the many duties of the household. For heaven's sake, the milk truck delivered 16 gallons of milk 2x a week! Next to the school we were the biggest order on his route. (I drank 2 gallons a week myself)

Some of our weekly responsibilities included taking turns cooking, babysitting, and helping with other various household chores. I'm sure that at the time we begrudgingly completed the tasks and probably would've preferred spending more time playing, but as the older children, we made it possible for everyone to to learn valuable life lessons and have fun while doing it. I loved to do the dishes, as we would have a water fight with the sprayer, and took out 2 birds with one stone because we also cleaned the floors by having to hose down the whole kitchen area. We were able to learn how to work hard, how to be less selfish, how to care for younger siblings, and how to rely on each other, and my siblings are my best friends.

I have always admired the love and respect that my parents have had for one another. My dad has stood faithfully by my mother every step of the way. He has been a wonderful and wise provider, a man of honor and integrity, but the most enduring quality is they both are our best friends, and they love us unconditionally. Sometimes we stray, make mistakes, or whatever the circumstance may be, or maybe we just have to learn something on our own and they are there to give us support, love and sometimes just that listening ear of a loving parent that helps us know it is going to be okay.

We will never tire of listening to Dad's stories of the scriptures. My parents continue to persevere in spite of whatever may plague them at this time with age, broken hearts for their children, broken pipes, or you name it, they've seen it. Even though they face many challenges and trials in the process, they continue to teach all the rest of us even more about faith, endurance, and determination.

My parents continue to serve and have undertaken inner city missions, temple service, and more in sharing with others their mortal experiences that sometimes in darkness it helps bring us to understanding, finding and experiencing true happiness and lasting joy.
* Anyone who has been around my parents for long, has unmistakably observed that they are the quintessential essence of hope, light, and love.*
They are truly an example of pure love, generosity, and kindness.
Their sacrifice and Love have allowed them to bless the lives of our families, and of many people; and so it is with all of us if we are willing to have hope, courage, and determination to keep on going.

I was watching my parents interact at the hospital on one occasion when my father was in for open heart surgery It was a tender moment and it was something I will not forget during my mortal existence (as long as I keep my faculties anyway)

Mom:	*"I love you!"*
Dad tried to say"	*"I Love you More"*
Mom:	*"I love you the Most"*

Dad: Trying to say "I love you the Mostest

Dad almost ripped the tube out of his throat to top it!
My Grandma Neta had a saying as my parents are alive at the time of this writing and think might appreciate it.

"Spread it thick… like honey on bread!
"Don't wait to spread the BULL"
"Til After I'm DEAD!"
`*~Grandma Neta~*

We can start spreading now that we've shared the facts!

Grandma Neta's little sayings:

1-You are not a darn site better than I am to work
2-Choose Wisely because your decisions are brief but endless
3-You may fly around the roses but you could land in the manure
4-A job worth doing is a job well done
5-Where there is a will there is a way\
6-Fix it up...Clean it up...Wear it out...or do Without
7-Take Freedom away and what do you have...Mere Animals
8-No deal is a good deal if you can't afford it
9-If you are going to do the job, do it right or don't do it at all
(My Saying: Anything worth doing is worth doing again)
10-If a dog bites you once... it's his fault, dog bites you twice it's your fault
11-Worrying is like a rocking chair...back and forth back and forth but gets you nowhere
12-Many Hands make light work
13-Many a slip between the cup and the lip
14-If you don't like my gate, don't swing on it
15- The size of a man's nest egg depends on the chick he picks
16-A person convinced against their will is of the same opinion still

~MP~
CHAPTER 17

**HEALING: The other side of the veil
Nora Burnett**

~Contribution~
Nora Burnett

My son passed away at the age of 26. He ended his life after suffering with severe mental illness. He had been diagnosed with many mental and physical debilitating disorders: bi-polar, severe depression, extreme anxiety, borderline personality, ehlers danlos syndrome, paranoia, psychotic, Asperger's, schizophrenic and fiber myalgia. He also experienced opioid addiction. Towards the end of his life, he was in so much mental anguish and physical pain, there was no Doctor, Therapy, Psychiatrist, ECT treatment or ER that could ease his torment.

Now in hindsight, I can finally see this to be true, even after going over it in my head a million times as to what I could have done to change the outcome, as his Mother and caregiver. On a day to day basis, my husband and I would never know what each day would bring. We loved our son and tried desperately to be good caregivers. It seemed we were constantly fighting an uphill battle that could never be won.

Many times, my son would beg us for our help, and we would try to do all we could, then we would start to feel manipulated and then feel guilty for not meeting the endless needs of the "black hole" he felt inside, a black hole that could never be filled to what truly plagued him. Then there were the times we would back off, realizing we were trying too hard to rescue him and creating more problems. We wanted him to be self-reliant and safe and not depending on us for the rest of his life. With his mental and physical disabilities, we tried to teach him the skills and tools he would need to help him function on his own. Then often times it seemed his situation would go from bad to worse and we would step in and continue the cycle of rescuing.

As a caregiver, one of the hardest things for me was to watch my son suffer through the decisions he made or wouldn't make because of his disabling illness. If there was anything I could do to help, I would try to do it, but I had to learn the hard way that there is a fine line between healthy care giving and rescuing. Rescuing can be enabling. I have since learned that rescuing can often take away a person's agency to act for him or herself for opportunity to grow.

There were also those times when my spouse and I were not on the same page as to what would be best for our son and that usually led to marital stress and division and created a negative effect on the whole family including his other three siblings.

There were hopeful times, times when we would start to see the light at the end of the tunnel. Seeing our sweet, fun loving son start to take hold of his true potential and accomplish his goals; for he was very gifted. We wanted so much for him to be happy. I am so grateful for the good times we shared and I will always hold them dear in my heart.

Being a caregiver, I always did better when I was getting enough sleep and eating well, which I honestly did not do all the time, sometimes I let stress get the better of me. When I did take better care of myself, there was more of me to go around, and I could handle life a lot better and I might add, a little chocolate can go a long way too! Writing a daily journal or log for my son was always helpful. I could go back to a certain day and see how he was doing behavioral wise or what medication might be affecting him. It helped a lot. There were times I needed "just me time" or time to get away with my husband or sisters. It made all the difference in the world!

In closing my contribution to this amazing and healing book, I would tell you (the reader) never give-up for the person you are care giving for. Even though my son is not here, I know his spirit has moved on. I am a Christian and I know that this world is not the end. I know I will see my son again and that brings a great deal of comfort and Joy to my soul. I know he is working on things there that he wasn't able to do here.

~AP~
CHAPTER 18

NOT THE GIGANTIC TITANIC
Grandma Jelly's Atlantic Crossing

Edmonde Fuller & Grandma Jelly

Atlantic Crossing -The Olympus

New Era 1978 by William Hartley

[Retold by (4X Great Grandson G. Burnett]

As anxious European Saints crowded aboard the beautiful sailing ship Olympus, an apostle prophesied that their voyage would be terrible—but successful.

Elder John Taylor, presiding over the French Mission, was in England on Church business in early March 1851. He took time to bid good-bye to friends—converts and missionaries—then leaving Liverpool for America aboard the

Olympus. One friend was William Howell, who the previous year had opened up France for the preaching of the gospel, and who was named presiding elder for the 245 Saints taking the trip. Elder Taylor wished the travelers well. Then he

prophetically warned that the Olympus would be wracked by storms, that Saints would suffer from evil spirits and from sickness, but "that God would preserve them in the midst of all dangers, and lead them to a harbor of safety."

Sailing time to New Orleans was normally about five weeks, ocean conditions permitting. Hopefully this company of Saints, departing March 4, would reach America by mid-April so they could travel up the Mississippi River before the spring and summer months brought killer cholera epidemics to that area. This, the seventh Mormon company to sail during the 1850–51 emigrating season, would be the last one until the following January. Captain Wilson, an expert seaman, commanded the Olympus, its crew, the company of Saints, and the nearly 60 nonmember passengers.

The troubles predicted by Elder Taylor suddenly struck during one of the first nights out. Below deck nearly 400 souls were asleep in the tightly stacked berths along each side of the "extensive bedroom"—about 30 yards long and 8 wide. "In the dead of the night" a 13-year-old lad excitedly leaped from his bunk and at the top of his voice screamed over and over again the name of a fellow passenger. The boy's parents and a brother and sister could not silence or subdue him. "It soon became apparent," noted passenger Wilson Nowers, "that he was possessed of an evil spirit." Through the administrations of the priesthood, the evil spirit was dispelled.

Another part of Elder Taylor's prophecy likewise found quick fulfillment. Hardly had the Olympus entered the terrible Irish Sea when harsh head winds whipped huge waves against the wooden vessel day and night. For three weeks many of the tossed-about passengers were seasick, "suffering intensely from the distressing affliction." Finally, when a calm day brought relief, the passengers felt the worst part of their voyage was behind them. But Captain Wilson's trained eyes, making a careful survey of the horizon, spotted a rapidly approaching cloud. At first it was no bigger than a man's hat, but it swelled and spread at an alarming rate.

Quickly the captain massed both shifts of the crew on deck and ordered all sails immediately shortened. He allowed Brother Nowers and a 20-year-old carpenter from Dover, Edmund Fuller, to stay aloft and help the crew. (Later in the voyage Mr. Fuller fell in love with a Mormon girl, Adelaide Jelley, and he joined the Church and married her in St. Louis.)

Barely were sails hauled in and secured, and passengers herded below deck, when the new storm struck the ship full force. The Olympus trembled and reeled "like a drunkard."

The "regular white squall" snapped the foremast off and carried it overboard. Several men nearly went overboard with the broken mast, which, hanging by the ship's side, had to be cut loose from its stays with axes. Torrents of wind and water sprang the mainmast at the deck.

*Thrown on her beam ends the Olympus became
unmanageable. Into a fearfully dark night the ship
struggled, battered by hurricane winds. Seams of the
vessel cracked, letting water seep into the hold.*

*Two hours after the storm began, about 8:00 P.M., four
feet of water had poured into the hold and the ship's
pumps were started. Above, knee-deep waters rushed over
the decks, causing Brother Nowers and Mr. Fuller to lash
themselves to the pumps they were manning to keep from
being washed overboard. Hour after hour the storm raged.
And the Olympus took on more and more water.*

*By midnight the captain, crew, and men on deck were
despondent because the storm showed no signs of abating.
Within earshot of Brother Nowers the captain ordered
Second Mate Hamilton to go below deck and tell the
Mormon's president, Elder Howell, that "if the God of the
Mormons can do anything to save the ship and the people,
they had better be calling on him to do so." The captain
confessed that despite the crew's best efforts the Olympus
was sinking at the rate of one foot per hour and that by
daylight it would be on the bottom of the sea unless the
storm ceased.*

*The second mate asked Brother Nowers to accompany him
below to deliver the message to the Mormons. As soon as
the crashing waves allowed, the two messengers unbarred
the*

*companionway and ducked below. They found Elder
Howell in his bed and told him the captain's appeal. "*

Very well," answered the Mormon leader calmly. "You may tell Captain Wilson that we are not going to the bottom of the ocean for we embarked from Liverpool on a voyage for New Orleans, and we will arrive safely in that port. Our God will protect us." Mr. Hamilton returned to the deck and gave Captain Wilson the Mormons' answer.

Brother Nowers, dripping wet, could not help noticing the absolute chaos below deck. Everywhere unsecured trunks and packages rolled and skidded from one side to the other as the ship swayed and rolled. Some passengers were crying. Others prayed. Still others simply waited.

President Howell quickly arose, dressed, and called about a dozen brethren, including new convert Wilson Nowers, to his side. The leader instructed that each man in the circle take a turn to pray vocally that the Lord would spare the vessel. Elder Howell prayed last.

"While he was still engaged in prayer," said Brother Nowers, "I noticed a material change in the motion of the ship." Instead of rolling and pitching, the Olympus "seemed to tremble as one suffering from the effects of a severe cold." He could not believe the ship was sinking. But he also could not believe that the storm had so suddenly ceased.

After the final hearty "amen" President Howell sent the prayer circle members back to bed. Brother Nowers, however, returned to his pumping duties on deck. There, astonished, he found that "the storm had miraculously ceased; the wind had gone down, and the waves were stilled immediately around the ship, while in the distance the billows were still raging." The Olympus trembled at so sudden a change.

Pumping continued until daylight. When the Sabbath day finally dawned, clear and bright, Captain Wilson admitted that he had done all he could do before calling on the Mormons and that only God's hand had saved the sinking ship.

While sailors rigged a jury mast to replace the broken foremast, passengers crowded onto the deck. Saints and nonmembers joined together in prayers of thanksgiving. The passengers put on clean clothes, and for the first time since leaving Liverpool, newly shaved faces appeared. A delegation of Saints obtained Captain Wilson's permission to hold Sabbath religious services.

That day, March 23, after sermons and hymns, a baptismal service was conducted. During the three-week voyage a number of non-LDS passengers had been converted and wanted to be baptised. The captain gave approval for a large water barrel to be brought out on deck, the top removed, and short ladders placed beside and inside it. The barrel was filled waist deep with sea water. Twenty-one persons, male and female, were then baptised. The next day the converts were confirmed, the sacrament administered, and the sick anointed.

During the voyage the Saints' exemplary attitudes and conduct worked to good effect on others. Nonmembers attended the Saints' 10:00 A.M. and 9:00 P.M. prayer services and the regular preaching services at which five or six brethren delivered short addresses. They witnessed meetings where spiritual gifts—prophecy, speaking in tongues, and healings—were evident. They and their children attended the Mormon day schools and listened to evening lectures by elders on various secular topics. Such contacts with the Saints produced more conversions.

At the second baptismal service 20 males were baptised in the ocean itself. The ship's main hatch cover was suspended by ropes on the Atlantic's surface to make a floating platform. Then, Counselor Smith and others sat on the platform with legs in the water, having a safety rope around their bodies. Each convert descended to the platform

by rope ladder, with safety rope around the body and a stout belt around the waist. He sat to the left of the elder officiating, who grasped the belt around the waist by the right hand, and the clothing at the back of the neck with the left. The candidate's hands grasped the elder's wrists. Then the person "was placed beneath the briny wave and brought forth therefrom." By the time the Olympus' passengers disembarked at New Orleans in late April and took the steamer Atlantic to St. Louis, 50 of the nonmember passengers had been converted and baptised.

At St. Louis the company split up. Some sought work there. Others boarded the steamer Statesman for the 13-day trip to Kanesville, Iowa, where 150 LDS wagons were being readied for the first trip west for the 1851 season. The final missionary success of the Olympus Saints came when the Statesman's cooks and deckhands, impressed by the goodness of their LDS passengers, left the boat en masse at Kanesville, intending to cross the plains and become part of the LDS society in Utah.

~AP~
CHAPTER 19

SAVE save SAVE!
When 1 and ½ bushels = 90 bushels

Record of Keziah Miles Goodman Warner Maw and retold by Great, Great Great Great Grandson-From Her Bible journal

I, Keziah Miles Goodman Warner Maw, was born on May 2, 1834 in Hallaton, Leicestershire, England. I joined the Church of Jesus Christ of latter-day Saints and was baptized March 4, 1854 in England.

I left England, November 22, 1854 on the ship," Clara Wheeler." After we had been at sea for a day and a half a terrible gale came up, and the captain signaled for a pilot and he took us back to the port where we had to wait several days. However we were not allowed to leave the boat. During our stay, there were 21 couples married on board ship and I was one. I was married to brother William Warner of Glooston, England. We held a fast day and prayed and the Lord did stop the storm and the Saints again started out. It took us six weeks after leaving Liverpool, England to reach New Orleans.

The next day after arriving in New Orleans. We took a riverboat up the Mississippi River to St. Louis. It was very cold and they were cutting the ice on the river. We spent Christmas day on board the boat.

On January 17, 1855. We reached St. Louis and then had winter for sure. I and the women stayed there until the following April, when brother Warner and brother Miles Andrews with others went up the country to get work. Later I went up the Missouri River, where some of the sisters to Atchessions camp. There, with many others, I took the cholera and was very sick for a long time. Many who took it died. One of the brothers sent for brother Warner and he cared for me until I was well again after I recovered. He went to work on the farm. There until 25 July, then we restarted with ox teams to cross the plains.

We were the last company of the season to cross the plains. There were 50 or 60 wagon loads are oxen were very wild one day an Indian came up with his bright colored blanket and frightened the first team. This started, all of them running and stampeding. A boy fell out of the wagon and was killed.

During our travels. Many took sick and died, and we had to bury them by the roadside, many of the oxen died also, and we were forced to leave some of the wagons behind. Before we arrived at our destination. Our supplies ran low, but Brigham Young, who was expecting us, for out manned and provisions to meet us

We arrived in the Salt Lake Valley, November 1, 1885. I had to remain in Salt Lake for three weeks, while brother Warner and others went back to get the wagons we had to leave behind. By this time, winter was drawing near, and the grasshoppers had eaten up most of the crops, so provisions were very scarce and hard to get. But brother Brigham Young for us and brother and sister Stolworthy on the church farm up to cache Valley, which is between Logan and Mendon. Sister Stolworthy and I were the first white women living in the cache Valley. Sister Stolworthy had the first white child born in cache Valley, which was a girl. If I had remained there three weeks longer, my eldest boy would have been the first white boy child born there.

There were lots of Indians and squaws there and just us two white women and seven men. All the others took cattle and horses down the river bottoms for winter. Pres. Young told us to be very kind to the Indians and feed them or else they would kill us. This we did till we had almost nothing for ourselves. We only had very little wheat left and were snowed in the Valley with no cattle or horses. We used to grind the wheat in the little coffee and make gruel out of it to make it last longer.

After our wheat was gone, we didn't know what to do so one young man named John Dowdle said he was going to settlement for supplies or die in the attempt. He had to cross the mountains and the country all on foot, which was very dangerous for wolves and wild Indians alone. The friendly Indians told him not to go or he would surely die, but he would die anyway, so with our faith and prayers, He started out.

He arrived all right for the Lord blessed him in a few days, he returned on a mule with a sack of flour. It was a long [dangerous] trip for one sack of flour to be divided among so many, but it was the sweetest and best flour any of us had ever tasted. He had many wounds on his legs, were wolves had attacked him. As soon as possible Brigham Young sent us more flour. We were rationed to 1 pound for each man, and 1/2 pound for each of us women. We had nothing else, no butter, milk, or vegetables, but plenty of beautiful water, for which we were very thankful for. Out of many little share, I used to save one full cup full of flour a week.

Brother Warner, and I left cache Valley for Ogden on 22 July. Up to this time I had saved 23 pounds of flour out of our share. Had I not done this. I should have had a bit when my first baby was born three weeks later, on August 4. We arrived in Ogden. By this time.
My husband works with brother Robson and received 20 acres of land and payment down in the forks of the Weaver River. It was covered with willows and trees which she had to grub off. That fall on a 5 acre field where the Union Depot now stands he and brother Robson gleaned wheat from which he had got one and 1/2 bushels of wheat. Then he cleared 2 acres of our own ground and plant that that one and 1/2 bushels of wheat. At harvest time. He got 90 bushels in return.

The next wall. My husband had to go to Echo Canyon to meet the Johnson's Army, who were coming to kill the Mormons. He carried his rifle, but he had no bullets. I, with my baby, was left in the little willow and he had built for a house.

Brother Warner had made the adobes and put up the walls of our little house, but hadn't gotten the roof on when the bugle called and he had to leave. Bishop Erastus being him for a man to put the roof on my house he put willows a mentor without windows or floors and moved in. Then there came a big rain and all the mud began to come through on my bed, so I got up and put the table slanting over the bed, then sat with the baby in my arms until morning under the table. The next day brother, Samuel Bert came and took me to his home
. Then he went and scraped the mud off my floors and fixed the roof again. I went back and stayed there till my husband came home. While my husband was away, brother Robson thrashed and cut our 2 acres of grain and we got 90 bushels of wheat out of one and one half planted. Then brother Warner came home from Echo Canyon and just got our ground plowed ready for the next planting when the heat came from Pres. Brigham Young – – – not to plant, but to get ready to move south. The army was going to pass through and brother young didn't think it would be safe, so he helped them back to we all moved south so our land had to be left unplanted

On the ninth day of April, we arrived in Salt Lake City. There, one of the brothers was leaving, so we took his home on the 11th my second baby was born while we stayed there, six other babies were born there was no doctor, a midwife care for all of our babies. From there we traveled to Summit, Sanpete County, and stayed there till 19 July and then came back to Ogden to our little house which we sure thought a lot of even if it didn't have any windows or floors

The first thing my husband did was to look at his farm and to his surprise he found a lovely patch of wheat nearly ready for harvest, which amounted to 56 bushels. This made 146, Bush bushels of wheat grown on 2 acres from 1 1/2 bushels planted. We surely felt blessed by the Lord. Brother Robson and family stayed for two or three years and we realized the good of all the grain. When he returned, brother Warner made it right with him.

Time passed until 1863, when my husband, brother Warner was working on the Ogden branch canal and a big cave of earth buried him to the waist with two other men (they were buried all over). Brother Warner wouldn't allow his fellow workmen to dig him out until they [tried to help] the other man out, who were buried all over. He stood the weight and the pressure of the dirt under his body so long that he was badly crushed internally and the doctor only gave him five days to [live]. But he lived 14 days. The other men lived many years after.

.Brother Warner died on Sunday morning, and as the crops had to be taking care of. They all got to work and made his [took care of his crops], and then closed that day and buried him and moonlight Sunday night. There was no embalming those days.

We were married on the scene and he was buried by moonlight. He was the fourth person buried in the Ogden city Cemetery. I was left a widow was poor little children, no relations in the country and a large farm.

After a time, brother, Charles Welch brought brother Maw (Edward) from plain city, Utah to visit with me and we became very good friends, and were soon married. He had a small girl about four years old named Alice, which I raised with my children. We live together about 30 years and six more children. When brother, Maw, to, was called by God on August 9, 1893. I was left alone again, but by this time my family was getting large, and the Lord blessed me and was with me at all times.(Signed) Keziah Goodman Warner Maw

~MP~
CHAPTER 20

DIRT-All families have it!

~Contribution-Mike B.

Dirt, all families have it!

I was fortunate and grew up in the perfect family! Loving parents, food and lots of dirt to play in and around.

As a young boy, I loved to be out and doing things. Didn't really matter if others called chores work or play. For me, everything outside seemed like play and everything inside the home seemed like work. Unfortunately, to those who wanted me to do chores around the house, it was their chore to convince me to work. Growing up I found conflict as a way to get out of housework. I think I had this weird idea where no one was going to pressure me into doing something I didn't want to do. It held fairly true growing up. I had brothers that beat on me to get me to mow the lawn and parents that unsuccessfully tried discipline techniques. I just would not bend to others.

My mother spanked me and I laughed at her in a mocking tone about how little it actually hurt. She gave up spanking me when she broke a hairbrush on my backside and after the use of a hanger didn't slow my mouth. I deserved a belt, but she never tried that.

My parents went to a teacher parent conferences and were told about how good of a kid I was. I had a teacher that lavished praise on me as I stayed after school in Jr. High to play chess with him. My parents wondered why I was so hard to discipline at home and such an angel everywhere else.

I had nine siblings and as an adult I know the house work required my hands to work as much as anyone else. One Saturday my mother had asked me to clear the kitchen floor after I refused to do anything else, like vacuum. Kind of odd to think she somehow felt giving me a harder job would encourage me to work. It didn't and I quickly let her know I was not going to do any of it. She tried grounding me and other threating tones to get me to engage in some work. I told her nope and used my mocking tone to let her know she couldn't change my mind.

This particular Saturday she had a new approach to try. After some of the usual methods of encouragement she brought my grandma "Neda", my Dad's mother, into the discussion. She thought she would have some power of persuasion with me. I was known as grandma's "peanut", as I was affectionately called. I had enjoyed being around the ankles of my grandparents during the construction of several houses. My mother had been secretly discussing the difficulty in raising me knowing I loved to do work with her. Why – because the work always building something and usually out of the house

Just mentioning her didn't get me working so my mom picked up the phone and my grandmother came over immediately. As she began to talk to me, I used the mocking language I had used with my mother. My attitude shocked her and my determination not to do any housework. She began to cry!

It was wrong to avoid housework and I knew it. It was even bigger to reject the concern my grandmother had in being there.

What I didn't see clearly at the time was just how my actions affected others. Her last ditch was to entreat me with her homemade apply pie if I would do the work. I refused and she left for home crying and letting me know she cared about me and was disappointed. She also said, "The offer of a fresh baked apple pie stands if you change your mind".

My prior feelings were such that I was in charge of myself. Nobody could force me into anything. When it came to chores that got left undone, so what! But the tears weighted me down with an emotion I didn't like. After everyone gave up on me doing the chores, I got the bucket of soap and scrubbed the entire floor by hand. I thought I had made a valid point about not being forced into anything.

Years later I learned my grandma had a young extended family member who needed some parenting stay with her. Over time and consideration her and husband (Omer) decided they could not permanently adopt this individual who needed some parenting. She left their home after some struggles with disciplining her. The rest of this girls' life was not easy and she passed away in sorrows. My grandma let me know that not trying to do more for this individual was a big regret. When I learned about this story from my grandma I recognized what I had seen in her as she appealed to me to clean the floor. She cared! There were other emotions too, but no doubt she cared enough to have regret about her abilities to help someone else see things with a better perspective. A perspective that would allow for peaceful living.

My grandpa Omer was physically a strong man! Possibly the strongest I have ever known and even in his older age was an astonishment. He was also thought of by many as, "a gentle giant". His hands were strong, with wrists that were as wide as the average man's arm. He had worked for the gas company as a ditch digger. He dug ditches for piping using an old spade shovel and he had developed a talent to dig fast! At around 14 years old my grandma had taken me and a friend to work on a home to be remodeled. It needed a side porch entrance area changed to allow basement entrance without flooding.

It required a four to five foot dig downward into the soil. To accomplish anything while digging, we had to toss the dirt up over the embankment of dirt created by the digging. This was no small detail as the mound quickly exceeded our height as 14-16 year olds.

During the dig my grandpa had gotten the friend and I into a competition to see who could dig out a section of dirt the fastest. We aggressively shoveled and were so quick that much of what we threw up on the embankment came back down at us. Dirt also rolled back and over into where my grandfather was digging. I never heard a whisper of complaint from him as he encouraged us in this digging race to see who would be the best.

So here is what I remember about that day. My grandpa dug faster and more dirt than both of us could as an old man. He did it without complaint and encouraged us both to be the best we could be. Both I and the friend wanted to win. We wanted to win so badly that we dug fast but without thought or planning. I am certain my grandfather saw and felt our short comings as our dirt often tumbled back at him that we failed to fully throw over the embankment.

Funny thing was, he moved more dirt in less time than the both of us combined and still praised us like we were doing all the work. We knew what was happening and that was fun work!

I learned a valuable lesson from these two grandparents in their own ways of teaching. All of us in families or as groups have some dirt that spills back into the lives of others around us. In a quiet moment of reflection about caring for others I ask,

1 Have I shied away from needed work because what we know doesn't fit with who we think we are?

2 Have I been discouraging others with thoughts surrounding hardships and a desire for moral correctness?

Well I have seen the impossible happen! Youthful ignorance gave way to charitable reason.

Now I know that entreating with tears of concern and fostering encouragement with the dirt falling back upon me is often a lifting for others. I know because I have watched a young boy as stubborn as any mule move on their own to work. I scrubbed a floor and ate a homemade apple pie. I dug a ditch and felt validated for good work. Working not for the desire of winning, but in the caring and longer lasting prize of accomplishment.

Maybe the most important lesson, don't let the dirt falling into your life from ever rising embankments stop the work of building something with others. Share in a trial, stop worrying if you have a heavier shovel than the person next to you and get to an accomplishment! That's what those whom you love and work really want anyway. I can still taste the memory of that apple pie!

~*MP*~
CHAPTER 21

MANY HANDS MAKE LIGHT WORK`

~Contribution-Bonnie Chadburn.

Thankfully I've been born of goodly parents. They are as perfect as you can get. The greatest gift my parents gave me was life itself, along with nine other siblings who I enjoy being with. Since I was the oldest of the ten I did my best to set an example and be obedient.

I was born in the days when fathers were sent to the waiting room This really bothered Dad because he felt he should be with Mom. With modern policies this has changed for the better and the miracle of birth is a family affair. My parents were kept plenty busy bouncing and rocking their demanding baby. To this day rockers are soothing and fun to read in with sweet babies or even see them fall asleep.

Grandparents have played a huge role in developing my character and Grandpa Omer and Grandma Neta lived right next door much of my youth. The first day out of the hospital I was scooped up by Grandma and paraded proudly down the hall as she showed me off. She continued to watch over, teach and protect me and saved my life once when the car door opened and I was hanging out just about to land on the pavement.

Work and play was two ingredients that were lived on a daily basis by them both.Grandpa was strong and steady as an ox and babysat us as they put their shoulders to the wheel to remodel our home for improvements. As my grandparents aged I would take the children and we would sit beside and read family journals and were very close. The two of them served a mission in Canada with President Russell M. Ballard being there mission president.

They hit the newspaper as their faithful testimonies created a stir and was noticed. If a young missionary was homesick they were sent to my grandparents for a meal of homemade fruit canned by them, nurtured, and put to work cleaning the bathroom. This worked in almost every case. Work and laughter was the best medicine and Grandma had many sayings with one famous one being,

"Many hands make light work!"

Grandpa Pete was quite the inventor and it was a joy to see him create with wood things such as a footstool with storage. Many hours went into his towel bar and niterider inventions. (for reading with a light) At Boyle's furniture I got to work side by side with both my grandparents. Loyal customers would ask for Pete Boyle because they knew they were working with a man of integrity. He was a skinny spitfire with a sure testimony of the gospel that he was unafraid to share. Grandma Margie was infamous for her Sunday dinners and we would hang out by the phone praying that we would be the lucky family to feast at her table. Not only did she feed faces the soul was nourished as well. Many a conversation was had as we ate a delicious meal and strong ties were made with these treasured memories. Family Scriptures in the mornings and Family Nights with a talent show were big. Many a time we were uncooperative yet taking note just the same. There was great love in the home and whatever disagreements my parents had were resolved behind closed doors. My Mom would say,

"Use language of intelligence." This meant no swearing.

Who can say they never saw their parents swear or fight. This love carried me through some really tough times. Each of us have a cross to carry and one of mine has been a mental illness diagnosis-bipolar which manifested in my adult years after having children. The gift of my large family blessed me as they rotated and took turns watching over me. Over the years with medical advancements and as I have learned to be diligent with self care and seek professional help I am living a rich full life. The book I got to be the author of is

Illuminating Love In the Home-Spotlight on Mental Illness.

This was inspired by the light, hope and great faith that has been exemplified by my parents and siblings and the book shared with others who are suffering in this way with tips for caregivers too.

Let it be known that there is light at the end of the dark tunnels of our mortal existence and through the healing Atonement of Christ joy can be chosen in this life!

~AP~
CHAPTER 22

A FEW THINGS TO SAY ABOUT MOTHERS

& More

Contribution-A few words to Say: Grandma Vaneta (Neta) Burnett

MOTHERS

I would like to say a few things about Mothers and wives, mothers of our children.

From some point of view Mother's Day has more important events in our lives than another other day except Sunday. Our Mothers and wives have had more influence in determining the quality of our lives than anyone else and should therefore stand next to God in our affection and appreciation and honor we show. Napoleon was once asked what was the greatest need of France and he answered, "Good mothers. Let France have good Mothers and she will have good sons." By the act of thinking about, caring and honoring our Mothers, we lift ourselves up.

In President David O. McKay's great book, Gospel Ideals, he wrote…"Last night I dreamed about my Mother," and then he said, "I would like to dream of my Mother more often and relive those wonderful days I spent at my Mother's knee while I was learning from her the lessons of life that brought me to my present station. They were the lessons of honor, truth and godliness.

Our lives can be greatly benefited by remembering our Mother's trials and sacrifices for us. Whatever may have been said about the sins of the fathers, it has also been said the virtues of the fathers shall be visited upon the children. Thirty-four hundred years ago out of the lightening and thunder of Siani, God said, "Honor thy Father and Mother."

The Prophets have pointed out that the family must be perfected together. Parents cannot receive their greatest eternal glory without the children. Mothers cannot receive their greatest happiness either here or hereafter unless we as sons and daughters live godly upright lives

God has given us a plan. It was He who organized the family in the first place and told us if we would live right, the family could maintain its identity and unity throughout eternity. Certainly God was not thinking only of a few years when He said it was not good for man to live alone, and he set up in each of our homes a Mother to perform a special service for us on this earth. As we look upon her with love and honor, we tend to make her ideals and ambitions ours and we tend to establish a place in our lives for her. Our Mothers, whose body nourished us, whose loving arms sustained us, whose every thought was to help us to do and become what we should be.

She is our wisest counselor, our most effective teacher, our most faithful supporter, our best friend, our Mother.

Abraham Lincoln may well have been representing us when he said," All I am or ever hope to be I owe to my angel mother." I would like to read a poem.

The words that came to each child from the heart of his Mother.

Do you know that your soul is of my soul a part
That you seem to be filler and core of my heart.
None other can please me as you, dear, can do.
None other can please or grieve me as you.
Remember the world will be quick with it's blame.
If sorrow and shame ever darkens and covers your name,
Like Mother, like son is the saying so true.
The world will judge largely of Mother by you.
Be yours then the task as the task it must be
To force the proud world to pay homage to me.

Be sure it will say, when the verdict is won,
Be she ever so proud how this man is her son.
Talk about children…..
Every effort must be made to wisely direct children that they may be fortified to live well in this topsey, turvey world.
David O. McKay once said, "Mother in her office holds the keys of the soul and she it is who stamps the coin of character."
The older I grow, the more grateful I am for the life and influence of my Mother. Not just today but in past years. Mothers have always needed the patience of Job, the simplicity of Simple Simon and a sense if ginir to rear children.
Then I am reminded of the Savior when hung on the cross with his throat parched with vinegar looking down at his grief stricken Mother at the foot of the cross and at John his beloved disciple, He said, "Woman, behold thy son. John, behold thy Mother."
The mothers of today must realize that instinct does not furnish all the equipment necessary to meet her child's rearing problems and Mother's love is not an adequate substitute for knowledge and efficiency. She must make a scientific approach to her task of child guidance. She must recognize that divine wisdom must constantly be applied in solving her problems. She must wisely appraise her situation and earnestly try to preserve fundamental values.
Motherhood in Retrospect
What we make of motherhood in life depends on ourselves. The same skies that are dark to one may be glorious and blue to another. Many times in trying to grasp the material things beyond our reach, we leave unseen and unappreciated the many sweet bits of happiness that lie close to us.

I look at these young mothers and I know that their task is not easy. Though children bring their compensations and joys, looking back I know every mother experiences moments of sorrow, days of anxiety and great sacrifice and most of all great responsibilities. But as I look at these young mothers, I know they can and will meet the challenge.

Today Mother finds herself living in a world of confusion. She faces a streamlined speeded up world. The pattern of my youth was not the pattern of children and mothers today. My pleasures were found mostly in the home and small community and ward with a more even tempo.

Today my children and grandchildren are in high powered cars. They mingle with girls and boys who smoke and use alcoholic beverages that in my day would have made especially a girl a social outcast. Today these things are socially accepted by many people.

Economic problems today are pronounced. Living standards are growing increasingly high and human wants are astronomical. The simple things that brought joy to me would scarcely thrill the girl of today. The problems of bridging the gap between Mother and children, the task of meeting the economic needs , the difficulties in rearing a family in an atmosphere of kindness and affection in today's world are overwhelming. But I know you young mothers will be successful and merit the praise of the nation on Mother's Day and the respect and gratitude of those children whose lives you are molding.

We know the family unit is an eternal thing and family ties are sacred.

One of the greatest privileges which God in His kindness has granted us is that of bearing children, of mothering the spirits He created and has allowed to come here. But with this privilege came the responsibility of guiding these spirits into happy, useful lives, worthy of going back into the family circle of the heavenly home when life is done.

A Parent's Prayer

O Master, make me a better parent. Teach me to understand my children, to listen patiently to what they have to say, and to answer all their questions kindly. Keep me from interrupting them and contradicting them. Make me as courteous to them as I would have them be to me. Give me the courage to confess my sins against my children and to ask their forgiveness when I know I have done them wrong.

May I not vainly hurt the feelings of my children. Forbid that I should laugh at their mistakes or resort to shame and ridicule as punishment. Let me not tempt my children to lie or steal. So guide me hour by hour that I may demonstrate by all I say and do that honesty produces happiness.

Reduce, I pray, the meanness in me. May I cease to nag and when I am out of sorts, help me to hold my tongue. Blind me to the little errors of my children and help me to see the good things that they do. Give me a ready word for honest praise. Help me to grow up with my children, to treat them as I would those of their own age, but let me not expect of them the judgment and convention of adults. Allow me not to rob them of the opportunity to wait upon themselves to think, to choose and to make decisions. Forbid that I should ever punish them for my own self satisfaction. May I grant them all their wishes that are reasonable and my I have this courage to withhold

A privilege which I know will do them harm.

Make me so fair and just, so considerate and companionable to my children that they will have a genuine esteem for me. Fit me to be loved and imitated. With all Thy gifts, of great Master, give me calm, poise, and self-control. Amen.

Grandmothers

Life smiles as we advance in years and become grandmothers. Bryant Hinkley wrote, "Children interest me, challenge and fascinate me as nothing else can. My own children are boys and girls grown up and gone to their own homes. That's what makes grandmothers. But I thank the Lord for the shouts and laughter of grandchildren. Honest and industrious children are our most precious possessions. The future waits upon them, In their hands is the future, destiny of the world."

Allen Beck gives us the definition of a boy. I like it. "Boys come in all assorted sizes, weights and colors. Mothers and grandmothers love them. Little sisters hate them, big sisters and brothers tolerate them, but heaven protects them.

A boy is truth with a dirty face, beauty with soiled fingers, wisdom with bubble gum in its hair, and the hope of the whole future with a frog in its pocket. But he is grandmothers and mothers captor, jailor, your boss and your master, a freckled face, pint size, cat chasing bundle of noise.

But when you are home alone at night with only the shattered pieces of your hope and dreams, he can mend them with just one word, Hi."

Adversities when met triumphantly can breed in our children and grandchildren patience, industry and consideration for others. There is no Royal Road to achievement, no easy process for building character in our children and grandchildren. We need not seek it. It cannot be found easily but what do we get for nothing.
Nothing with a capital N.
Someone has said character is a hardy plant that thrives best where the north winds blow and is tempered with the sunshine. Great souls have come up through tribulation and not from sheltered ease.
It is the things we overcome that make us strong. That's the reason the Lord made the world hard. We do most for our children and grandchildren when we help them to help themselves, to become reliant, to make good decisions, to formulate plans and to walk alone secure and unafraid.
I want the world to love my children and grandchildren. I will always love them no matter what they do. I may not love what they do but I will still love them. But the world will only love them if they conduct their lives in a Christ-like manner. We grow old, years wrinkle the skin but to give up enthusiasm wrinkles the soul.
The only way we can avoid old age is to die.
There is nothing more refreshing than to have your children and grandchildren come dashing in to say "Hi."
All people want to be recognized. They want respect and consideration shown them. No one has the power to hurt you or to elevate you as your children and grandchildren. I would like to say if we would be happy, we make our home a center of hospitality. That is what being a grandmother means to me. I am only as happy as my unhappiest grandchild.
From George Q. Cannon, September 1, 1899, Juvenile Instructor

Extravagance is the sin and peril of the age. Either from the example of others, or the laxity of their own principles, people are prone to live beyond their means. What ever they earn they spend more. Debt is easy to fall into, but its slavery is terrible. It discourages ambition. It is a drag upon high endeavor. It is slow but consuming death to an honest and sensitive soul. War hath slain its thousands but debt its tens of thousands. It makes of him whom it catches in its toils a serf and either a coward or a scamp. It grows like canker, it burns like caustic, it grinds on and on till the grave closes over its unhappy victim. It eats relentlessly any of his substance not only while the world is awake and active, but also while all the world sleeps. No lock or bar can keep out its blight. In no clime or concealment can the debtor escape it clutches. To earn a little and spend a little less means contentment.

Courage in facing one's fellows incentive, to bravely struggle with the world's adversities and honor and reputation of the most priceless sort. Peace of mind is a jewel beyond compare. Whether it be associated with wealth or poverty or be found in that genial middle zone where contentment with a little holds sway. But debt is a tormentor and a mill stone about the neck and is the natural and sworn enemy of happiness. Shun it, reader, as [you] would a serpent.

***

Transcribed from her Standard Examiner Clipping]
A Letter to the Editor- Ogden Standard Examiner-

Class Suggestion

Editor, Standard Examiner:
 Regarding the recent controversy on sex education in our city schools, I feel that first of all, the "name-calling" could be eliminated. Second, if all persons concerned with the subject would read the article in the Nov. 15, 1966, issue of Look magazine entitled "Sweden's New Battle Over Sex," it will tell what 10 years of sex education have taught such things as abortion, contraceptive uses, venereal disease, etc. By high school age, student[s] regard pre-marital relations as natural and acceptable. Contraceptives can be purchased by anyone from automatic vending machines available at all hours. However, some of the kids are not motivated to prevent pregnancy nor VD. Today Swedish experts are baffled by the increase in unwanted pregnancies and VD. The program is now being re-examined.
 ---Certainly we should avoid Sweden's mistakes. Let us hope the sex education program is not a fad such as the cigarette one and find 10, 20 or 30 years later that it was all a mistake.
 ---Some program is in line and could be taught in hygiene course would definitely be more but the impact of an intensive course woul [would] definitely be more harmful than helpful.
 ---And most certainly parents should have the privilege of deciding to what extent the program should be carried out for their sons and/or daughters
 V. Burnett

~AP~
CHAPTER 23

FLIPPED A CASKET

Contribution-Great Grandma
MARY ROSELTHA FULLER BURNETT

I, Mary Roseltha Fuller Burnett was born December 20, 1880, in the town of Eden, Utah, the first child of Henry John Fuller and Mary Jane Gould Fuller. I was blessed in the Church of Jesus Christ of Latter Day Saints and christened (named) February 3, 1881.

My first recollection of my life is at the age of five. I can remember helping my grandmother, Adelaide Jelly Fuller carry large buckets of food to the pigs and also playing with Aunt Edith who was then a child. I remember my grandmother's funeral. In those days the caskets were taken to the graves in wagons. The horses became frightened and jumped a ditch, throwing grandmother's casket out of the wagon. Naturally, I was anxious to see the results but my mother's warning kept me beside her.

When I was six years old I had the measles. My brother told me that since I was confined to bed he would bring a newborn calf to the window to show me. I waited at the window for some time to see the calf and in the meantime I was looking out upon the bright snow. As a result my eyes became weakened causing a nearsightedness, a handicap for me the rest of my life.

I attended school in a one room school house which was also used as a church, for social gatherings, and for civic affairs. A large round stove in which wood was burned stood in the center of the room to provide heat. My first teacher was Naomi Fifield, but previous to my schooling, Mother taught me my alphabet from the Bible.

The first day of school Mother bought me a second grade reader from the General Store because of my previous interest in reading and because I had had some knowledge of word recognition. I graduated from the eighth grade when I was thirteen years old. I attended the Weber Academy for three months, but didn't continue my schooling because of my eyes and my extreme homesickness. At the time I attended the Academy I lived in Ogden, Utah, with my mother's friend, Mrs. Lawson.

I was baptized September 5, 1888, (Eden Ward records said 1889) in Eden, Utah, by my father. At that time Fast Meeting was held on Thursday morning. I was confirmed the same day by James Burt Sr.

I seemed to be a very healthy child and was large for my age. I was one of the awkward ones, not very popular. I had mumps, chicken pox, and a cold occasionally, but no serious childhood illnesses. When I was about ten or eleven years old, my father bought an organ and I was given lessons by Mary (Mamie Littlefield), a young lady from Ogden, who was living with my father's sister, Edith. I enjoyed playing the organ and was eager to learn to play. At the age of twelve I was sustained as Primary Organist.

Our first Sunday School Superintendent, James A. Thompson, held what he called a Jubilee every three months, which consisted of singing, recitations and talks by the young members. He always gave me something to recite, for as he said, I could learn quickly and remember very well.

I recall when I was about ten years old, the Government Agents coming to the house to check on polygamy. They were inquiring about my Aunt Lizzie. (Elizabeth McBride, the second wife of Heber McBride; my mother's oldest and only sister) Aunt Lizzie's daughter, Nora, was living with us at the time while Aunt Lizzie was away trying to support herself and daughter. This visit was very upsetting for us because we had understood that the Agents were cruel men, who would do much harm. It was a relief to know they were only checking to see that people were living the Manifesto which was declared in 1890.

About this same time my brother, Willie, decided he was going to take us for a ride in the baby buggy with a rope hitched to it. However, before we got our ride the horse became frightened and ran down the road, kicking the buggy into bits. Mother was disturbed over the loss of the buggy.

Each year the Indians with their provisions strapped to their horses would travel through Eden to a new living quarters. Myself and brother and sisters would pretend to be brave and watch the Indian procession pass by. However, as the redskins would get within sight we would run into the house and hide. If any Indians came to our house to ask for food we would cling to our mother for protection. During the time I lived in Eden the Indians were friendly to the people with no outbreaks of hostility.

In my early days we had no electricity and used kerosine lamps for lighting purposes. It was my job to wash the lamp chimneys every morning, as they always got some smoke on them. We drew the water for household purposes out of a well with a bucket hung on a rope or chain attached to a windlass which was operated by hand. We also had a homemade washer which was operated by hand. After several years of use the washer wore out forcing us to wash on a scrubbing board. Our flat irons were heated on top of the stove. My father hauled wood or logs from the mountains in the winter and sawed and chopped the logs to use in our iron stoves. We had no bathrooms and our bathing was done every Saturday night in an old washtub.

The young people in the town had surprise parties and weekly dances as entertainment. The Mutual put on plays. I never had a chance to participate in them, but my father was in almost every one of them.

At the age of twelve I took my first long trip, my first train ride and experienced something few people had the privilege to enjoy. I attended the Salt Lake Temple dedication. I went with Aunt Lizzie and her daughter, Nora. We traveled to Ogden, a distance of twelve miles, by wagon, then boarded a train to Salt Lake. We attended the afternoon dedication in April 1893, and heard Brother Wilford Woodruff, the President of our Church, give the dedication. This was an all day trip and an enjoyable one. Although it took us a day to make the trip by wagon and train, one woman in Eden, Mrs. Johnson by name and a convert to the Church, would carry her baby and walk to Salt Lake to every conference, a distance of over fifty miles; truly a faithful, sincere woman.

There are many experiences of my childhood which I can recall, but they seem unimportant to place on paper. I led a normal life with a spiritual family, father being Bishop. My mother was mother to eleven children, eight girls and three boys. Willie, the oldest boy, died at the age of seventeen, October 23, 1900, and the ninth child was born a few hours later (Arvilla).

The young people of the town had dances and parties to which I was invited. James Burnett asked me to one of these affairs and then was called out of town, James sent his brother, Matthew, to escort me to this particular party. This led into a courtship of one and a half years and marriage on January 26, 1899, in the Salt Lake Temple. My Aunt Lizzie made my dress. It took three weeks to make it, but it was beautiful and was used as a costume for many, many years. Our first home was the old Burnett house which was later destroyed by fire. Three years after our marriage we built our home in Eden. It was a two-story brick house, large rooms, high ceilings and six rooms. We lived there for many years and it was a home that held many pleasures for my family.

I have worked in most all Church organizations during various times of my life. At eleven years of age I was Primary Organist; May 19, 1895 to July 15, 1900. As 2nd Counselor in the Primary Organization; August 11, 1900 to June 16, 1907. As 1st Councilor in the Primary Organization from June 1907 to October 30, 1910. I was Assistant Secretary in the Sunday School; September 7, 1902 to October 30, 1904. I was a teacher in the Sunday School; October 1912 to April 24, 1913. I was class teacher in the Relief Society April 24, 1913 to February 12, 1914. Then I was 1st Counselor in the Relief Society. Since that date, I have spent the rest of my time working in the Relief Society Organization either as a teacher or Counselor. After my marriage, we lived on the farm approximately a mile from church and I drove a horse hitched to a bum to all my meetings, sometimes with one small baby in my lap and four to six children beside me.

In the year of January, 1911, my father contracted typhoid-pneumonia and died January 13, 1911. My mother had been very ill for several months, but she seemed to receive strength and took care of Father. My mother contracted pneumonia and died January 20, 1911, one week after Father. My father was born December 18, 1857, at Mill Creek, Utah of English descent. He held prominent positions in the Church and in Sunday School. He was Counselor to President David 0. McKay's father who was at that time Bishop of the Eden Ward. He (my father) was Bishop of the Eden Ward for sixteen years, until his death. He lived the life of a true Latter-day Saint and was respected by all who knew him.

My mother was born December 18, 1861, in Salt Lake City, Utah and just three months after her mother arrived in the Valley. Her parents arrived September 13, 1861, with the Homer Duncan Company. See Journal History of the Church. My mother's family moved to Eden when she was a child. Her mother died when she was eight years old, making it necessary for her to make her own way in the world. Her father married again and the stepmother was very cruel to the children.

As a child the meals consisted of one large bowl of gruel or mush in the center of the table and one spoon was passed around to each member of the family to dip into the bowl. This made Mother ill because of the unsanitary method. Her stepmother taunted her with the fact that she thought she was better than the others. My mother states that the stepmother threw her(mother's) little brother down the well and only by his clinging to the racks and pulling himself to the top was he saved. The stepmother also hit mother on the head with a hair brush, knocking her unconscious for several hours. Once while the father was away from home, the stepmother locked all the children in the cabin and set fire to it, then went to the hill to watch it burn. Fortunately a neighbor saw the burning cabin and saved the children. Kind Mrs. Eggleston took my mother to her home to raise her after she found Mother chained to the bedpost, bleeding profusely from a cut throat. The act was caused by the stepmother.

Mother stayed with Mrs. Eggleston until her marriage to Father, January 8, 1880. It was because of my mother's unfortunate experiences that she was very weak in body, but never the less a very humble woman. She always trusted in the Lord and was very active in her Church duties.

In my own family of boys and girls we had the normal troubles accounted to any family. We had our good times, our suffering, and our usual mishaps. Omer had his arm nearly cut off by a mowing machine when he was a small boy. A doctor was called in to sew back the arm and it was without any anesthetic. Omer also got his thumb in the derrick pulley. Adrian had his appendix removed and each year a minor accident occurred.

Because of the large farm, we had hired men which necessitated cooking three meals a day. I did all the baking of bread (8 to 10 loaves a day), pies and cakes. I used a coal stove. I did my own canning and one year I recall canning 25 bushels of peaches at one time. Electricity was brought into our home in 1924, and in that year I had my first experience with an electric washer and electric iron. On July 3, 1916, our tenth child, a son was born. The doctor was drunk when he came to deliver the baby, and I believe, cut the cord too short. The baby became very ill and passed away July 16, 1916. I have always said he was the tithing to the Lord. Previous to his birth, I had a dream that two babies came down the elevator in the Temple, one was dark complexioned and one was blond. The blond baby went back up the elevator, but the baby with the dark hair was happy to stay. It was shortly after this that my sister had a dark complexioned baby, and my tenth child was blond, My sister's baby lived.

In January, 1920, a flu epidemic hit every family in the town. My husband had a herd of cattle in the lower valley and had gone there to take care of the winter feeding. My entire family of six boys and five girls were all down with the flu a whole week. It kept me busy going from one bed to another administering to their needs. Three or four were seriously ill. Merlin, my oldest son, would get out of the sick bed to milk the cows and feed the cattle. At one time I felt that I might be coming down with the flu, but my prayers offered to the Lord for strength to aid my family were answered and I felt the weakness leave me. I called in my uncle who was then Bishop to administer to the family and by the power of the Priesthood and our faith and prayers the family recovered.

In 1924, we bought a house in Ogden, Utah. My sons kept the farm. We resided at 2323 Monroe Blvd. and while there, we managed through the depression years in spite of the large family plus boarders. My husband worked hard all his life to till the earth and to provide. My husband passed away September 2, 1944, of leukemia and my oldest daughter passed away October 13, 1945, of surgical pneumonia.

My sons and daughters have held responsible positions in the Church. The boys have gone right up in the Priesthood Quorums from Deacons to High Priests, working as teachers, Sunday School Superintendent, MIA Superintendents, Bishops, District Presidents, High Counselors and Stake Missionaries. Harvey went to the California Mission, Adrin to the West Central Mission and Ivan went to the Mexican Mission. My daughters have all held responsible positions in the Church and attended their Church duties faithfully.

On June 29, 1928, I had surgery to remove a tumor and on January 13, 1954, I had surgery for a perforated ulcer and three-fourths of my stomach was removed. It was only through the prayers of the family and the Priesthood that I quickly recovered so that at the age of this writing I can still be of some use to the world. My hobbies are crocheting and piecing quilts [in] which I enjoy.

—

Great grandson:
[
I got that taken care of and then ran to the side of my many cousins and siblings playing by the river bank I believe the big family reunion was at North Fork camp grounds where we jumped the river and chased frogs. It was beautiful and we all were having such a wonderful time when…
KABOOM!
Lightning struck a very tall tree right by where we were enjoying the picnic. You know how you can tell how far away the strike was by counting
1001 – 1002 -1003… ETC.
Well there was no count, but I remember looking over at my sister and laughing because her long hair was whirling up and around and there was a funny feeling in the air just before it happened that I now know was static electricity.

It split the tree nearly in half and fortunately for everyone and everything was okay, but that was the end of the reunion as we were rushed to the car and the sprinkles turned from large intermittent drops to a major downpour. My great grandmother made me a spunky monkey with the assistance of my aunt Mardel). I believe it is still with us a and half a century old too. They knew how to make quality gifts of quilts or little animals, and I loved my little stuffed monkey.

~AP~
CHAPTER 24

BIG FOOT - SHOE PROBLEMS

Contribution- Great Grandpa
William Van Dawson Burnett

William Van Dawson Burnett was born April 10, 1846, in Bulong, France, a son of David and Isabel Ruxton Burnett. David Burnett, his father was the son of Alexander and Margaret Robertson Burnett. His mother, Isabel Ruxton was the daughter of Alexander and Mary Watt Ruxton.

During the war of confusion, in Scotland, David R. Burnett and Isabell Ruxton moved to France with their children. On April 10, 1846 in Bulong, France, David R. Burnett rang the bell at the office of Doctor Van Dawson. A servant Girl answered the ring, but David Burnett being Scottish and not having been long in France, could not speak the language and so made signs to her indicating that his wife was going to be sick and wanted the doctor. The girl, not knowing what he said, slammed the door in his face. He went home and made signs to the landlord of the house and she understood and got the doctor, but the baby was born before the doctor got there. The doctors charges were nothing, only the name, and so it was christened in the Book of France, William Van Dawson Burnett.

A war broke out in France and all foreigners had to leave in 1846. William Burnett was only a few months old when they went back to Scotland. His parents had earlier joined the Church of Jesus Christ of Latter Day Saints around 1840 in Scotland. The name is Bur-nett, French or English, but it is originally Scottish pronounced as Burn-it with the accent on the first syllable.

When 14 years of age, William Burnett emigrated to America with his parents. He was baptized into the Church of Jesus Christ of Latter Day Saints in Brooklyn, New York, in 1860. They started to cross the plains to Utah in 1861 with Jobe pinery handcart company. William's mother pulled a hand-cart all he way across the plains. He had one brother and a sister that came to Utah with them. As to how many brothers and sister William had is not known for they were scattered about in different states and nothin has been heard from them.

William's father hired him out to an old man and his wife named Bottles in crossing the plains. All the clothes he had were on his back except a pair of pants and a pair of hard leather shoes. The shoes got wet the first day out and the next day he threw them away because he could not put them on, so he went the rest of the way barefooted. In a few days William's feet got sore with stone bruises [on] each heel. He traveled 20 miles on the tips of his toes for two weeks. He forded every river and mud hole crossing the plains, barefooted, leaving blood tracks in the snow. Before he reached Utah, his pants were worn off the knee. The sun blistered his shoulders until they hurt. He slept on a stove all [the] way and had a cheese box for a pillow. He was then 15 years old. He was tied to a [pair] of cows that were not broken, so that they would not get away from them. He had a
straw hat which was worn out all but the crown. He was burned from the top of his head to his feet. He suffered a great deal of pain. when he got to Green River, he gave out and fell down, but stye told him he would still have to walk. The cords of his legs hurt painfully. He felt the punishment of [the] Job. His father and family were ahead of him and he never saw them until he reached Salt Lake.

His father, David Burnett work[ed] as a guard at the penitentiary under A.P. Rockwood, one of the first guards of Utah. they rented a [farm] and made a good many gallons of molasses on share that fall. His father then hired him out to Winslow Farr in Cotton Wood. He told a great liking to William. His folds then moved to Tooele and he was hired out to a man named Pickett to [herd] sheep for a code of steers in exchange for a years work. he gave the cattle to his father. His father, brother Dave and himself built a water wheel to grind molasses and then started work getting out lumber to build a mill. They were all to be partners in the business. William worked in the canyon barefooted and lived mostly on nettles and greens. Flour was hard to get. It took three of them to bring a load of wood to the saw mill. One to take rocks off the road, one to drive the cattle and one to pound the tires from coming off. They got the mill running and made molasses, but they split up the partnership. William's mother was sick for a year and had to be taken care of. She was fed Laudanum to ease her pain.

They were all worn out from sitting up with her. She died sitting up in an old arm chair where she had spent most of her invalid time. She was buried in Tooele Utah. Later the graveyard was moved and his mothers grave was plowed up. He was then 18 years old. He became acquainted with Sarah Jane Wilde who was also an emigrant to Utah. She came from England in 1863. She was two years older than William. William and Sarah were married in Tooele city by Bishop John Rawberg on Jan. 25 1866. They were remarried by George Q. Cannon in the endowment house in Salt Lake City and sealed for time and eternity Dec. 7, 1866.

They had a son, john who was born before they were sealed in the Endowment House. When he was born, they never had a stitch of clothes for him. William got his father's team to haul a load of wood and started to Salt Lake City to get some clothes. From now on he tells the story himself..........

I never fed my horses, being in a hurry to get back with the baby clothes, and when I got half way the horses balked in a salaries bed. I unloaded the wood and carried every stick on my shoulders a block. I then loaded up again. I had not gone a mile when they stopped again. It was then ten o'clock at night and freezing hard. I threw it all out of the wagon, but they still wouldn't even pull the empty wagon. I went to their heads to lead them, but they reared up and pulled my shoulder out of joint. U then uncoupled the wagon and pulled it out myself, two wheels at a time. I then loaded up again. I went two miles and it was getting daylight. I went to cross a pond of ice and half way across the wagon broke through. I went a mile to barrow an ax to chop the ice and get my wagon out.
 I finally got to the city and sold the load for $4.50. It took me four days to get the wood and make the trip. I bought 4 yards of material, a bunch of buttons and a spool of thread. Today I can get the baby dress for 75 cents. I lived with father when I got married. I never had a five cent piece. I got some slabs, made a bed stead and used straw for a mattress. we had a wagon cover to cover us and no pillows. The only light was the fireplace. I had made a candle, but a dog stole it.

All we had for clothes was on our back. All the furniture we had was some boards for a bed stead, two stools, and a black skillet. I kept a soldier coat for a pillow. My wife had her pretty coat. That winter we lived on beet molasses and a little bread.

We were very happy in our log cabin. My brother, Dave was then guard at the penitentiary. He wanted me to guard with him. I sold my cabin and lot to my father for a span of horses and wagon in the fall. Later I sold my horses for two cows. We moved to the pen under A.P. Rockwood. We were there for two years and were paid three dollars, a day in store pay and fifty cents extra a night to sleep in the cells every other week to save expenses so they wouldn't have to hire an extra guard. it was dangerous work. I have had some very narrow escapes from being killed. One prisoner drew a gun at me.

I had to finally let him go. another time two stage robbers were going to kill me. We were working in the canyon south of Camp Douglas. they were making roads and cutting brush. They all had sachets. Tom Moore was with me as guard. I was laying down when one of them came up and choked me. He took my gun and ran to help the other robber. That was on Moore. I had a shot gun concealed in the brush. I fired at the one on Moore, and shot him in the leg. The one that got my gun, ran. The gun wouldn't go off. I tried to shoot the other barrel. The cap fell off. I had a small five shooter in my boot.

While he was running, I fired it at him. He was quite a ways off, but he bullet struck him and killed him. I did not like to do this, but it was my duty. My oldest, Sarah was born at the penitentiary on Sept. 9, 1868. We were living in the Sugar House Ward. I went to work getting out rock for the temple from Cotton Wood Canyon. I worked one summer there. I had saved $50 while at the penitentiary, so bought a span of ponies and moved to Harrisville. My son David was born here in a house rented from a man by the name of Rayer. I temporarily moved to Liberty to get out a set of logs to build me a house in Farr West. Liberty was then a wild country. Indians would camp by my house. Bear prowled around. Rattlesnakes and mountain rats would scare my wife.

In the fall I moved to Eden. I had 8 bushels of potatoes to start on. I moved in with Dave Eccles. That was a hard winter for me and my family. There was no work to do that winter. My wife would sell what little things we had in the house for a pound of butter. Dave Eccles' mother would sometimes

bring us a little meat. My wife often fainted for something to eat. However I paid my tithing to Bishop Ballantyne and when spring came, I never owed any man a dollar. The spring of 1871, I moved to Farr West to build my house on my land. My brother came to see me, but found us so poorly fixed that he went back to Brooklyn, New York. Without equipment to fence my land, etc. I was in a poor fix to farm, so I concluded to go work in the mines in Cotton Wood Canyon to earn enough money to start farming. Here I made three dollars a day and sent it all home to my wife. While I was gone, my son Dave fell down the well head first and lit between two rocks. Later I got word that my son, Will, almost got burned to death, so I came home again. The pigs and chickens had frozen to death. I almost got discouraged.

My wife bought a pair of shoes, munger9, too big. When we went to Ogden, she carried them under her arm and went barefooted. Then she would put them on when she got to the bridge going into Ogden.

When she came home she should take them off at the bridge and walk home barefooted, a distance of 8 miles. I later worked at the railroad and worked getting out quarry rock for the building of the temple for tithing pay. Things began to pick up and so I traded my farm land in Farr West for 160 acres in Eden. I let my father and his second wife, Sarah C. Kitterson live in my house in Farr West. He lived 16 years on it before he died and I buried him. His second wife lived three years longer. Ogden Valley was a herd {[hard] ground for people to turn there cattle out. Their cattle broke in my field day and night. Because of these condition five or ten acres were fenced by the people as a stray pen. I would put these stray cattle mint he pen [in the pen] and then get in trouble with the people for doing so. My farm wha stye [was the] first farm to take water with the Water Co., As I had one of the oldest farms in the Valley. John Frichet built a mill below my farm and Dave Eccles' father took out a ditch above the mill. I could only get water when they let me have it. I had trouble from then on in one way or another with water and the court suits over it. even when the law seemed to be on my side, some of the men would lie before the judge about my rights.

I now had 320 acres from the Rail Road Co. which owned the land. I was hard up. I had to borrow my seed to put in a crop. I had a fine crop of oats but the grasshoppers came and destroyed it. It was a hard struggle to pay for my land, as I had no earnings except hauling a load of wood once a week, most of the men in the valley earned third by doing this at that time. In 1880, I put in my crop again. I had a fine crop,

after fighting the stray cattle and people for my water rights. The grasshoppers came again and were eating everyone's crops. They flew over my field. I thought it was my turn next.

I was in debt for the seed. I threw a stick at the grasshoppers and [in the] name of the Lord said, "get out of here". IN a little while, I went out. There were no grasshoppers to be seen. Everyone's crops in Eden were eaten up. I raised 700 bushel of grain. The Lord was on my side with all the dirt work they tried to harm me with. I was getting older and tired of all this fighting for my water rights so I decided to sell out to my boys. I moved back to Farr west. There my wife died, Feb. 24, 1911.

I finally sold my farm in Farr West to William Gould for $7000 and went to Utah Hot Springs to work for $40 a month. I was there three years in the summer time. I came to live with my daughter, Margaret [in the] winter time. This is as far as Grandfather wrote of his life. It is told by one member of his family that at onc time, one of his boys was sliding down a hay stack and hit a sharp hay knife, cutting a large gash.

Grandfather took the boy and sewed it up with a needle and thread. While he was in Eden he had a son Tom, 19 years of age, dragged to death by a runaway team and wagon. His daughter, Clara pope and her twin boys died at the twins birth. Another son, William who was married and had a little boy died suddenly in his sleep one night. Grandfather always played with his grandchildren whenever he came to visit them.

Toward the end of his life, grandfather had neuritis for three months and suffered painfully.

He died Dec. 26, 1921 at the age of 75 years. He died the day after Christmas and was buried in the North Cemetery of Eden along with his wife and some of his 14 children. He died at the home of his daughter, Alice, at 359 Kershaw in Ogden.

~MP~
CHAPTER 25

THE ROCKET ROOST

A Nephew's Recollection

Aunt Pauline was a wonderful person and had a beautiful smile. When the cousin's would visit our house for breakfast they always said homemade pancake syrup was better. When I was seven three of my siblings and I tried to run away and our confidant was Sandra her daughter. We became cold and tired and tried to hide in Pauline's basement pantry. Sandra had multiple helpings for dinner and Pauline became suspicious that something was up so We were told to leave the house and hide in the backyard and allow Dan age 4 to find us. He found us hiding in the "Rocket".

Pauline brought us in the home and made sure we were safe and then called our parents and sent us home. Pauline's home in her latter years was directly behind my parents home. My parents and her would have many meals together and would check up on each other daily. Pauline made special effort to attend my children's musical recitals and events. She would bring fancy cupcakes to our Memorial Day bar-b-cue's. We enjoyed being invited to dinner in her home and were amazed at good the food was. She had a wall in the dining room with a tribute to her family members who served in the military. Dan the one who found us hiding being the crown jewel, Colonel Burnett. She was a wonderful aunt and I was great full to know her.

Dave. B.

I was also her attending eye care doctor and she was a model patient.

~AP~
CHAPTER 26

LOVE AT HOME
G. Roai Burnett

MODERN PIONEER CONTRIBUTION
LOVE AT HOME

Gary Reed Burnett

Mother

I have observed how Heavenly Father is quite reserved with what He shares about our Heavenly Mother.. I am reluctant in expressing these thoughts and emotions , but feel they do need to be said to my wonderful mother.

On the cover of my book is a small little hand claspping hold of his mother's hand. I beleive I remember being that little baby in your arms and the cute sweet soft noises and whispers you would make in my ears that would put a smile on my little newborn face ...and no it was not GAS! (Well okay, maybe it was, but a little of both.

Because of your loving embrace the security and love that I was able to have growing up was almost unreal. I felt so comfortible and loved in this world, it was very pleasant and I had a very easy going disposition. Now as I am in the world, I realize what a gift that was, and also how richly blessed I was to the point I was almost not ready to handle such a punishing and mean world.

When I left home I did fell armed with a knowledge and testifmony of a living Savior that you and Dad helped me attain at a very young age of 12 years old.

I recieved that beautiful Book of Mormon with the gold leafing around the pages, and after a week of intense reading, I could not put it down. Tears flowed from my eyes as Alma was forced to watched his loved ones burn at the hands of evil men. Nephi, and the struggle with his siblings, moving, and of coarse inspiring me to live in a tent for consecutive 40 days and 40 nights, and 100 days in a year not too long ago to see how it feels. And by the way, it was really nice. Probably way nicer than what they had to deal with. Neverthelss, a new and wonderful adventure.

I was able to find out that it does not matter where you live, but how you live. I was able to enjoy homes through my life, and was greatful for them, but I was just as grateful for the canvas roof as well. Just different materials, but all were welcomed and it was wonderful that you were able to teach us the difference between a house and home, and thank you Dad for providing Mom the necessary abundance for her to build and create and turn a house into a home.

I also appreciate that you shared the story of our friends coming over to play at our house because their mother was so maticulous that she would not let them play in her imaculate home. In later years her kids grew up and didn't come around much, and she was so lonely, but her house was microscopic clean.

Thank you for sharing that we want to have our home so clean that we could invite the Savior in, but not so clean it chases the spirit away, and thank you for the quiet room. A place that was always ready for guests, or we could go to have quiet reverent time to think or ponder.

Love at Home, A wonderful song that we enjoyed and sang at the church roadshow, and I still remember the new plaid flare legged bell bottom pants you got us (Cant wait for that to come back in style again...NOT!)

.Music and art filled the room along with babies, babies, and more babies. I enjoyed every new addition. Some may think I didn't enjoy maybe a sister or so, but they would be wrong. I enjoyed all of my siblings and am so grateful to be so richly blessed. My mother gave birth to 10 beautiful and fun new bundles of joy and they were all wanted and welcome, and I have to admit they are so cute! Every one of them! Myself included! LOL (I love myself... I am the best... to hec with him (Lou-or Lucifer).. and all the rest (of his followers). Thank you for giving each of us a solid relationship and understanding that we are children of God and are of a royal heritage. We learned that at a very young age.

Thank you Mom.

I had the coolest mom in the whole world and I got to share her with my friends as she was my Den Mother. She was the best Den Mother in the whole wide world! (at least in my opinion). The world of creation was opened to us and I loved my new pocket knife, that carved out the fantastic and intrique little buffalo soap carving that took 1st place. I would venture to say that it would rival even in the adult world. There were the coolest rockets in the rocket derby which fueled my passions for flying, and the pinewood derby was always a treat.

Dance was kinda fun as my brother was enrolled to help him get a little bit better coordination. I understand a little bit more as Dave turned out to be a GIANT, and it was funny because when we were running together in high school I would have 2 strides to his one. He made it look effortless with those big strides. I had to work twice as hard, but it was so nice to have such a good brother and friend by my side pushing...nope ... wrong word... coasting me to better times and greater heigths. I got to stand on the potium quite a few times.

Music filled our home and I loved when you guys provided us with a guitar and banjo from a Mexico trip. (Along with a fun chess set that we couldn't wait to play our Dad. He was REALLY GOOD! At least we thought so.

I remember when the piano came into the home and it looked too complicated and intimidating. but I remember Mom in her curlers, sitting at the piano and plunking out a toon or too, and eventually getting lessons so that I was amazed at how fast she was able to learn. In short order she was quite a pianist, and by her example of consistency and determination shared her talents with her family. (Thanks to Dad for providing the instruments. I understand it was Dad's idea and just showed up with it one day) Mom asked "Who is this for? cause nobody plays the piano?" Dad's response was, "Somebody will some day."

I think every child can plink out a tune, but most are insanely talented. I have to laugh a little because I am not very good, but who would of ever guessed that I am a piano teacher today, and love to help others learn and grow, and music is such a wonderful way to do that. Especially the piano as it will be beneficial to whatever music direction you go. This gift of music has allowed enjoyment in band, violin, harmonica, trumpet, baritone, recorder, drums, banjo, guitar, ... well I could go on and on. The world is an open book and if it is an instrument, can't hardly hold still. Just like to pick it up and play.

2 things that were definitely **not learned** from Mom was **driving**, and **swimming**.

Mom didn't drive until I was about Jr High age and was kinda forced into it out of necessity as we were building a house, and Grandma needed her to drive. The other was swimming. Now I had a fear of swimming until I got down to Lake Powell with the in-laws and they were all water dogs so one time when we were on the lake, I was told the wet suit I had on was special. It had materials equivelant to a life jacket in it so that I would not sink. I was not concerned that the depth of the lake was hundreds of feet deep because my brother-in-law said you can drown in a bath tub, You'll be okay. It doesn't matter if it is 2 feet, or 200. Just stay on top and breath and you'll be fine.

I jump out of the boat with this "special" wetsuit on and sure enough I can float, so I tell him to go ahead and put my nephew in and I will assist him in getting his skiis on and help him learn to water ski for the first time. Well he got up and down a few times and then they came back and picked me up. When I got in the boat they informed me there was nothing special about the wet suit, and I had been out there treading water the whole time. I freaked out and it was a good thing they waited to tell me after I got in the boat. After this experience they coaxed me to jump off the super high dive, and I looked down at the little people, and said, "I don't swim." They told me " No worries, just hold your breath and you'll float to the top- 2 kicks and your over to the wall. Sure enough, they were right. I lived and even jumped in and learned to SCUBA DIVE.

FATHER

As the world gets busier and noisier, it becomes critical for us to carve out time for those things that are of greatest importance, and from my vantage point My Father always put us at the front of the line whenever there was that option.

Bing a father is the toughest, but most important job I will ever have on this earth.

One day I was having a conversation with a friend that had been through a divorce as well and she shared these thoughts from a woman's vantage point that gave me a new perspective to think about. I had been murmuring a little about monies paid out that I didn't even have, and I greatly appreciated her gentle and kind remarks.

***

She Said,

"I understand the feeling about being just around to make money. Let me just share my feeling about that thought

-I think it comes from the adversary working on fathers. It is not that way.

Without money that family cannot have the physical surroundings to lead a spiritual existence. If a women feels she cannot rely on her spouse for the basics of a roof over the famiys head and food on the table, she has a hard time trusting him in other things. You have no idea how scary it is to have a little one in your arms that needs your mothering and you have no time to hardly think or sleep and then you have to deal with the fact that your spouse won't work. What it feels like is that the family has no provider or protector.

Ive been there more times than I care to think.If you think of the money as providing a foundation of security for those wonderful kids of yours, it will change your viewpoint. Security is what they need from their dad and money is half of the equation. The other is love and it sounds like they let you know that youre doing a good job in that arena. It takes kids feeling secure to get them to feel anchored and trusting in God. This is why the security a father gives to the family by providing a living is so important to the relationship a child has with God.

Your X may learn to appreciate you if she works full time, but she may not too. I dont understand a lot of the craziness women seem to be going through regarding the home and family and Having to work to meet their own needs.

Unless they get some easy job, theyll find its a dog eat dog world. To make enough to support my family, I have spent many years being the only woman in board rooms, the only woman who wasnt invited to the big boy golf tournaments where they decided the fate of my job with their fraternizing. Most of the women who say they want to work, only want an outlet, but they still expect their X or spouse to provide for the family. I wonder how it would feel if they HAD to make enough to support their family.

They would find the work world a bit harsher place. "

*** THANK YOU FATHER

I have found these words to be very helpful in taking care of my family. It was no easy task, and I am quite sure that the people on the other side of the fence were having a hard time understanding what I was going through. This brought great insight.In later years, we recieved further clarification when the **Proclamation to the World"** was released and gives some very important instructions to each family member of responsibilities and duties. I thank my parents for being such good examples and for a father that I NEVER heard complain about his duties as a father., and provided that security to his family in an exemplary way.

We love our parents. dearly. Your lives have blessed our lives! My most favored PIONEERS. Thank you for blazing the TRAIL for us. From all your kids:

WE LOVE YOU!

~AP~
CHAPTER 27

Saving the prophet's father
Matthew Burnett

Contribution- Great Grandpa
Matthew Burnett
- Saving the prophet's father

One of the most well-known stories about Matthew Burnett is how he saved David McKay's (the prophet David O. McKay's father) life. David McKay was heading home to Huntsville one stormy night. The river in Ogden Canyon was very high and swift; the roar was deafening. Brother McKay pulled his team over to let Matthew pass by with his wagon.

David got too close to the edge and the wagon tipped over, dumping him into the swirling waters below. The swift current carried him down, slamming his body into the rocks. He finally caught hold of a large rock in the middle of the river and managed to pull himself up unto it. In the meantime, Matthew Burnett was plodding along, letting the horses have a loose rein because they could pick out the road better than a human in these stormy conditions. He had his coat pulled up and his cap pulled down to keep out the cold. He thought he heard someone, but with the roaring water, he wasn't sure.

A voice came to him and said, "Go back. There is a man in the river." He untied the team, unhooked the mare and returned to where he heard the call. He saw Brother McKay on the rock, waving his arms. The river made a big turn above the rock where the water washed around it, and the bank was very steep. Matthew went up river and made the horse jump in the water. The force of the water carried them downstream to the rock, finally pressing the horse against the rock long enough for Brother McKay to climb on.

As the horse started to swim, the current carried them to bank of the river near the road. The McKay's wagon was nearby with his team standing close to it. Brother McKay later said that when he climbed up on that rock, he knelt and prayed for some way to be rescued. This was the moment that Matthew had heard the voice telling him there was a man in the river.

~MP~
CHAPTER 28

Modern Pioneers- Write you Own Story

COMING TO A BOOK NEAR YOU!

The end

~MINI LIFE LEGACY~

Game

(L&L 20 Questions to build a Strong Story)
Only answer the questions with responses you are comfortable in sharing (fun, little snippets that may help others (Avoid negatives unless you have a strong solution, then by all means share! Powerful!)
After playing & jotting down ideas from the game, a good way to start the **MINI LL** is:
A-PROBLEM: Identify common PROBLEM others can relate to and may be struggling with as well
B-STORY: Tell Brief STORY -(make a connection – but just enough-& not too Graphic-make connection)
C-SOLUTION -(SOLUTION you LEARNED or DISCOVERED that helps the reader move forward)
*Your story is GREAT-This is fun with a group of 2 or more people and a little timer***

2 Min. Response time per Q Approximately 1/2 Hr+ or (speed round 15 min.) Jot down /record responses
Lets have FUN!   Thanks for Playing!
1-*Born and Raised & How you got your name*
2-*Family: Kids/Bro/Sis Par &*
Gr/Cousins/Nieces/Nephews/Ancestors/..
3-*Holidays/Special Events:*
4-*Food Favorites-(To Eat &Make) -Recipes*
5-*Church: callings/leaders/scriptures/conversion story/life tests.*
6-*Love &Friends: close, old, new, young, financial, gone, Animals / Pets*

7-*Entertainment/Travel: Travel/Toys/memorabilia/ games /-(night/board/card/movies)*

_8-Health & Wellness / Illnesses /Meds/ Drs/
Nutra/Pharma/Patients_

**9-Success &Celebrations/Failures/Problems
Solutions, and Learning**

_Opportunities/Forgiveness : ex. Child/grownups/
authority/$/friends/law_

10-_Service: Missions / Community / World /
Military_

11-Attitudes / Theories / Quotes

12-_Mentors / Coaches /Talents
/Skills/Instruments/Music_

13-Edu. _/Schooling: El, Jr., HS, College,
Teachers/Principles/Adm_

14- _Likes / Dislikes / habits /patterns /exercise
/discipline/ affection /Passion_ **(LOVE)**

_15-Groups & Org.:
Running/Band/Scouts/Rep/Dem etc_

16-_Jobs & Careers / Businesses and Associates
/Trade_

_17-Cars and vehicles owned:
motos/snowmo/boats/tricycles/bikes/wagon_

_18-What is your Y (What is your purpose- Your
mess is your message)_

19-Change: _If you could travel through time
(past)P-P-F and change ?_

20-_What ? Do you need to add to this list to make
it complete?_

***ENDING WITH A TESTIMONY OR
PERSONAL THOUGHTS IS ALWAYS NICE**

**Senses: (taste, sight, touch, smell, sound to
describe and enhance your story)**

Proof